Riding with Jim is a great collection of stories and poetry. Andy's love for his dad, family and traditional values shine through on every page. This is great reading...

~Don Edwards, cowboy balladeer and historian

To all of us out there that are trying so desperately to hang on by our fingernails to the West and its lifestyle and values, help is on the way. Andy Nelson just tossed us a life jacket. His book, *Riding with Jim*, assures us that the "word" will continue to be passed along. In prose and poetry Andy introduces us to his family and friends, all of whom are living "the life." The intangible qualities of the land and the people that have made up the West. He captures the art of subtle humor in all his work. He makes you want to tuck in at the supper table and say, "Please pass the potatoes and Andy, tell us another one." You keep writing Andy and we'll keep hanging on.

~Alan Geoffrion, author of *Broken Trail*

Andy Nelson and I have romped around the Western entertainment circuit for some time now, and I've had the chance to see how his words and performances affect those with Western sensibilities. As the relatively new genre of cowboy poetry grows and evolves, I've always thought of Andy as one of its first adults, someone who brings more than just boilerplate campfire stories and rodeo yarns to the eyes and ears of Western aficionados. His poetry and stories are sharp, hilarious and meaningful, and his new collection, *Riding with Jim*, introduces an inspired conceptual component, the combination of prose written by his late father James Nelson with Andy's unique poetry and observations. The result is an important new book for those who understand the cowboy's West as well as for those who've not had the pleasure. *Riding with Jim* personifies the Wyoming Life, complete with nature's beauty, spirited horses, ranch life, cowboy geniuses and fools, and life's little vagaries. But ultimately, it is Andy Nelson's remarkable take on the precious and perfect concept of family.

~Jon Chandler, author of *Spanish Peaks*

I've been Baptized and Chastised,
Socialized and Civilized,
Criticized and Demonized
and that is just the start.

I've been Surprised and Despised,
Immunized and Patronized,
Terrorized and Tranquilized
and that near stopped my heart.

I've been Journalized and Compromised,
Recognized and Hypnotized,
Supervised, Mobilized, Fertilized
and Well Advised.

But through this book I Realize
that Andy Nelson's Country Wise.
His little book will Brighten Lives
for those who have been Andy-ized.

~Waddie Mitchell, buckaroo poet

Riding with Jim

Adventures with Cowboys and Farriers

Cowboy Poetry and Stories by
Andy Nelson

With Select Stories by
James F. Walker Nelson

Illustrations by Bonnie Shields

Pinedale, Wyoming

Riding with Jim
Adventures with Cowboys and Farriers
By Andy Nelson

Contact:
Andy Nelson
Post Office Box 1547
Pinedale, WY 82941
www.cowpokepoet.com
andy@cowpokepoet.com
(307) 367-2842

Printed in the United States of America

ISBN (13 digit): 978-0-9706459-5-1
ISBN (10 digit): 0-9706459-5-3

Contents

Poems by Andy Nelson
Stories by Andy Nelson and by James F. Walker
Nelson where noted.

About the Author

Photo by Amy Nielson

A second-generation farrier, Andy Nelson was raised in Oakley, Idaho, and traveled the Great Basin of southern Idaho, northern Utah and northern Nevada with his father on farrier jobs, from the time he was a child until he went off to college. While in college at Utah State University, he continued to shoe horses for the USU Horsemanship Program while studying in the pre-Vet curriculum. Now Andy lives in Pinedale, Wyoming, where among other things, he and his wife Jaclyn raise horses and children.

Andy and his farrier brother Jim co-host the "Clear Out West (C.O.W.) Radio" weekly syndicated radio show, and the brothers are in demand as announcers at regional rodeos.

Acknowledgments

Special thanks to:

Tennessee mule artist and mighty fine friend, Bonnie Shields for lending her tremendous talents on this project. (www.bonnieshields.com)

Photojournalist and lifelong friend Stuart Johnson for the book cover photo. He is one of the very few people in this world that can make me look almost life-like. (http://web.mac.com/swjohnsonphotography)

Amy Nielson for the great promotional photos. Not only is she a wonderful photographer but she is also my niece... poor kid. (www.amynielson.com)

The Center for Western and Cowboy Poetry preserves and celebrates the arts and life of rural communities and the real working West. It is the reason classic cowboy poetry survives today and is the inspiration for thousands of contemporary cowboy poets to preserve the art. Through projects like CowboyPoetry.com, Cowboy Poetry Week, and the Rural Library Project, the Center serves as a gathering place where all are welcome, all are accepted, and all are encouraged. The Center's managing editor Margo Metegrano, is a friend beyond measure. She is a sounding board, she is a confidante, she is in a large part why we write. A simple "Thank you" is never enough for what you do for all of us, but it will have to do for now until you are better paid. (www.cowboypoetry.com)

Dedication

To Dad

James F. Walker Nelson
1920-1993

I thrive on the back of a horse,
unlike the average man;
I walk only when I have to,
and I ride because I can.

Preface

My dad, James "Jim" F. Walker Nelson, (the "F." because he never cared for the name Francis), is a driving force behind my writing. An old cowboy and farrier, Dad loved to read and write stories and poetry just for the sheer pleasure of it. With no aspirations of being published or making money, he simply wrote for his own therapy. He loved his horses, his cowboy life, and like most old cowboys, he subscribed to the philosophy that a good wreck must be shared with others.

Dad taught me to be a horseman first and a farrier second; he always believed this was the proper order. He taught me respect for the horse first and then to insist on respect from the horse second; this too was the proper order. But the most important lessons taught to me by my dad came in the form of single-sentence proverbs. No lectures, no sermons... just simple, easy-to-understand statements that left no doubt in a young boy's mind. For instance, once while riding with Jim, the horse I was on busted in two and the last bit of advice I remember hearing was, "If you stay on top, you won't get hurt." After I was day-lighted and was lying on my back looking at the sky, Dad rode up with this positive affirmation, "You sure enough made the eight seconds." Both instruction and encouragement came in short sentences. There were also times of reproving in which he'd say, for example "If you are going to do stupid things, you'd better be tough."

I sure do miss having him around, but as I sifted through stacks of loose-leaf, wire-bound, and typewriter paper, *whatever Dad could find to write on,* I re-lived wonderful memories and experienced some never-before-told tales. I was reminded of how all Dads' cowboy friends used to call me "Little Gus" when I was a boy, because I was named after his father, Andrew Gustave Nelson. And now as I build a fire in his old forge, I draw on his experience once again. As I teach my children horsemanship, his instructions to me ensures their progress. As I struggle underneath a snotty horse, he still stands by my side issuing confidence.

Dad may have shuffled off his mortal coil, but he lives through the stories he wrote in the following chapters that begin, *"Written by James F. Walker Nelson."*

Andrew G. "Little Gus" Nelson

Riding with Jim

It's been years now, and I can't tell you how
many times I've wanted to rewrite the end;
I fret and I ponder, most often I wonder,
if I'll ever be as good a cowboy as my friend.

Friends come and go, as does every foe,
but certain people touch your life forever;
Jim was a horseman, unlike most men,
and a better farrier I've never seen, ever!

He was old and grizzled, and his blood sizzled
if I wasn't paying attention to his advice;
He taught me all, that he could recall,
about horses and shoeing, at least twice.

But I was young, and awfully high strung,
I didn't have time to listen to his stories;
I had to ride fast, and not be the last,
to taut my accomplishments and glories.

Of coarse I wasn't one, to ever be out done,
I was so full of myself, cocky, and young;
I knew it all back then, but that was when,
my wits weren't near as sharp as my tongue.

So I did my own thing, never wondering,
what was missing in my life back then;
It wasn't 'til later, my ego would crater,
and I would become teachable again.

My oats I kept sowing, not ever knowing
God sent him to make me a better man;
So He took him away, one cold spring day,
and I was left alone to do the best I can.

I never did think, he'd die on the brink
of me becoming the cowboy that I should;
But now it's too late, I'd sealed my own fate,
I'd have to venture alone into manhood.

I knew that I, couldn't break down and cry,
or let the others see how deep I was hurt;
I felt ashamed, and myself I had blamed,
for this old hand that lay cold in the dirt.

Many times he tried, before the day he died,
to share what he learned from life's travails;
But I didn't take time, my life was mine,
what could I learn from his stories and tales.

Well, now I feel cheated, for the way I treated
riding with that old cowboy as a chore;
And still I pray, that some how, some way,
I could ride with Jim just once more.

Periodically I'm given, a chance while still livin',
to ride horseback once again with Jim;
When I fall into a deep, almost comatose sleep,
God allows me a brief rendezvous with him.

I know it's just a dream, but to me it sure seems,
just as real as the first day we rode together;
We don't ever talk, we simply ride and walk,
enjoying the quakies, the sage, and each other.

We ride up Fall Creek, where the willows are thick,
and the untouched water cascades down,
A doe and fawn, bound effortlessly on,
we're partnered up and miles from town.

Then the sun peaks over, and spots this old drover,
and illuminates his face under his hat;
His peaceful look, like the cover of a book,
shows contentment for where he is at.

He is astride Big Joe, and we all know,
that big ol' steed was his favorite mount;
With his rawhide hack, and slicker on back,
we ride while cows and blessings we count.

As the dew burns off, I hear a cow cough,
and Jim sets out for the top of a draw;
I tag along side, our horses in stride,
and we gather that rogue without flaw.

We ride all day, gathering mavericks and strays,
and I know at any moment this will end;
So I hold on tight, this couldn't be more right,
but the home corral is just around the bend.

I don't want to wake, but as a new day breaks,
the stock's waiting for me in the morning light;
But first I thank God, and I give Jim a nod,
for the wonderful ride we took that night.

It don't sound like much, like a vision or such,
but it helps me 'til the next visit to be had;
And I'm proud to say, in a boastful kinda way,
that old cowboy was my mentor, and my Dad.

I took much for granted, but the seed he planted,
and now I cherish each and every ride;
My heart's still hurtin', but this I am certain,
Jim and Big Joe are waiting on the other side.

Speak Your Mind ...
and Ride a Fast Horse

Dad holding a thunder mug of "Pee-tunias"

So today I'll spend, trying not to offend,
with the things that I do and say,
As I ride and rope, I surely do hope,
for a politically correct day.

I grew up in the day and age of manners and respect for parents and elders. Now, I'm not saying that kids always showed respect for their parents back then, but what I am saying is if we were disrespectful, there were consequences. I know theories for raising children and training horses have changed through the years since the introduction of horse whispering clinics and children behavior modification seminars. The fact remained, if we goofed off, acted up or lashed out, there were consequences and we could not hide behind a diagnosis of Attention Deficit/Hyperactivity Disorder. We also grew up in an environment where adults spoke frankly one with another and did not worry about being politically correct.

Dad was an expert and could teach seminars on speaking your mind and did it in a matter-of-fact manner. The only problem, Dad did not possess the tact to pick the correct audience to showcase his talents *(that must be where I inherited the same trait)*. Dad was not allowed -- which was fine and dandy with him -- anywhere near when Mom's literary club met at our house. In fact, this is where I developed my flight response to the barn when visitors descend on my house. Mother was petrified that perhaps Dad might adorn the refreshment table with a thunder mug centerpiece sporting petunias, or as Dad liked to call them, *pee-tunias*. She was pathologically worried that Dad might cut loose with a limerick or other self-composed poem about a prostate exam, during a clergy visit. Mom's fears were justified, but did not seem to bother Dad nonetheless.

One of Dad's favorite past-times was to make stark, raving changes to the English language and insert them into conversation. This added extra entertainment value to simple conversation and his cowboy buddies depended on him to spice things up a bit, no matter where or with whom they were conversing. As young boys, big brother Jim and I would listen intently and soak up in Dad's vocabulary like a wool saddle pad soaks up horse sweat. And we were excited to put the new words into our meager way of speaking. Yep, the inherent problem was, there were no checks and balances as we implemented our new vocabulary in conversation with Mom. We could usually assess the shock value and how much trouble we were in by Mom's reaction. For instance, when big brother Jim responded to a question from Mom by stating, "It is *im-venereal* to me," rather than, "It is immaterial to me." She just shook her head and rolled her eyes in disgust and said, "Your father may talk like that, but you can't." Now, on the other hand, one night while eating supper, I wished to show my intellectual prowess by implementing a recently acquired phrase. To show that I was ready for the main course in our meal, I announced, "We are now ready for the intercourse." Mom's reaction was notably elevated after that one and my oldest brother Pat tried to cushion her response by assuring her the statement was out of ignorance, not arrogance, all the while unsuccessfully stifling his guffaws.

Other popular statements included: "Please bring me my spec-testicles" (referring to his reading glasses), "Pot-tunias" (flowers in a honey bucket), "Pootunias" (flowers in a bed pan), the previously mentioned "Pee-tunias," "Fart, fumble, and fall" (when one took a spill), "The Infernal Revenue Service" (self explanatory), "In the general vasectomy" (instead of vicinity), and many others that may be too ribald for the PG rated reader.

A Politically Correct Cowboy Day

Too brazen and bold, or so I've been told,
that my language is often perverse;
With crude words leaking, I've changed my speaking,
now it takes me all day to converse.

So today I'll spend, trying not to offend,
with the things that I do and say;
As I ride and rope, I surely do hope,
for a politically correct day.

I begin my day, forking off some hay,
then set a new dam in the ditch;
I run the calves by, with some help from my,
trustworthy border collie...
dog of the feminine gland.

With the cows and culls, the steers and the bulls,
I watch for what's left by the herds;
I walk through the yard, it gets kinda hard,
not to step in all of the...
mounds of bovine excrement.

I sweat and I toil, change my pickup oil,
and fill my shoeing rig with gas;
I've plenty to do, with horses to shoe,
and then go trim the neighbor's...
mule, donkey and/or burro.

I have foals to wean, the grain room to clean,
and repair broken reins and bits;
Bottle feed the lambs, and wether the rams,
rub bag balm on the milk cow's...
little hangy downy thingys.

I pound and bend nails, the work never fails
and I have a crick in my back;
My t-shirt don't hide, all of my backside
and I sunburned my exposed...
farrier's coin slot.

The work load goes on, been at it since dawn,
and I still have chickens to feed;
I've got fence to fix, some sweet feed to mix,
and the stud has brood mares to...
cover.

Without common sense, the stud jumped the fence
now I have to doctor his cuts;
While my knife is out, I'll turn it about,
and perhaps I'll remove his...
procreative privileges.

It's getting tougher, for this old duffer,
to converse without offending;
I can't say a thing, without wondering,
if a lawsuit may be pending.

So if you're annoyed, one just can't avoid,
when certain cowboy words may stray;
If my tongue may slip... I don't give a rip:
You just have a nice cowboy day.

The Roundup

Dad as a young boy, three years after the roundup,
with the horse given him by his father, Gus Nelson

It was as if virtue and vice
were drawn from the very same well;
Horse shoes attacking the pavement,
like Heaven had spilled into Hell.

Written by James F. Walker Nelson

We had our own Dust Bowl right here at home. When the drought was severe, Big brother Rex took four head of horses and went across the river on a road job. At home we scratched the soil a little bit with a mangy pair of older horses. Ironically enough, so dry as it was here, it rained and rained 70 miles away on the road job Rex was on.

The horses had to be fueled whether it rained or whether they worked, so Rex came home with two twenty dollar bills. At home we cut thistle weeds and stacked for stock feed, grew enough grain for flour and hogs. Having no money was inconvenient but lack of stock feed was a calamity.

After Rex had a day or two off, the three of us headed for the mountains for firewood and some young horses that were ranging out. There were two or three work colts that needed starting and two or three spring foals that needed branding. If one didn't keep new horse power coming there would be that inevitable day of being afoot. I rode a good bay bally (baldy) horse, of course named Bally.

We left the homestead early one morning we had loaded our supplies the night before. The bulk of the supplies was horse feed. One did not dare to hobble out 'cause we were going to the open country that these horses had grown up in, and should they get away your chances were mighty slim of seeing them again short of maybe a year or so.

We nooned at the forks of Trapper and Fall Creeks.
The wagons had to stay at Badger Gulch and over the
summit of Trout Creek. I had never been beyond this
point before. Dad brushed clear a spot on the ground
and drew a map. I was to ride Bally up Fall Creek
past a beautiful little waterfall and then proceed on
the ridges and peaks looking for horses. I was not
even to ride close to them but just locate them and
familiarize myself with the country. Man alive was
this great. I had no idea there was that kind of
country and that much country to look at. This was
early September and the weather, the trees, the
mountains were fantastically beautiful. I can still re-
live the elation in my chest.

Riding the peaks and ridges was play for the big
horse I was riding and all the while I was recording a
mental map; Dad had told me to always stop and look
back in order to know what the country would look
like when coming back. I saw three separate bunches
of horses and made a mental note of where they were
and how I thought I could find them coming from the
other direction. There were no fences. I rode in to the
Little Willow and then the Big Willows Creek
drainage. I recognized them very clearly from the
description and the map on the ground where we had
nooned. When Big Willow emptied into the bigger
creek that would be Trout Creek and up stream on
that creek I would find Dad and Rex with the wagons
camped on the downward side of a patch of big tall
quaking aspen trees. The sun was sinking and deer
were appearing out of nowhere... everywhere. The
onliest other time in my life that would compare with
that afternoon was a week at Water Fall Creek in the

primitive area, the identical time of year, when elk accompanied the deer at sundown.

The sun had disappeared but was still shining on the ridges when I located Rex and Dad. They had made camp and had supper going when I rode up, took care of my horse and saddle and very matter-of-factly reported. It took two days to load the wagons and get them out on top. They had to four up to get from the Quaker patch to the summit where we camped for the night. From the number of horses in the bunch and the location, Dad told me which bunch he wanted.

Dad and Rex left at daylight the next morning and I was to stall and locate my bunch of horses and merely appear where they could see me and then let them go unmolested for and hour or so. I was to ride around them a bit but always stay above. Dad and Rex had to be in lead and would have the gates open at the Trapper Creek Ranch corral. I located the horses and it was real difficult not to ride in Wild-West-like, but I had a profound respect for what my father told me. I did as told and the horse bunch became acquainted with me and continued feeding along. The hours went by like days. After the sun peaked and dipped well into the west I figured the time to be right. I got close enough to recognize a black mare and a buckskin mare and this was the bunch. They took off. I mean blasted off. This sort of thing was not new to the ol' gelding I was riding and he remembered to stay above them.

We railed brush and went through timber where I had to lay flat against Ol' Bally's side to keep from being scraped off. Somehow we all came out on the other side where the old smart lead mare was making a bid for the high country. Now was Wild-West-time all right. It took a mile or so of hard, fast riding to get the bunch headed downhill. The lead mare had made her bid and lost. She dutifully lead the bunch down to the road and on to the corral where Dad and Rex had the wagons parked to form a chute to the corral gate. Phew. What had taken hours to prepare for had climaxed in a matter of minutes.

I learned more on that trip than one can imagine. We branded the foals using a running ring and ran the neighbor's iron on his, kept three of the two year olds and a strawberry Sevina stud colt out of the buckskin mare, then opened the gate and let the others head back for Marlborough country. I couldn't dare to hope for what Papa had in mind for that beautiful painted horse; sure enough he was mine. I may have got some sleep that night had Dad waited 'til morning to give him to me.

I should mention here it was customary and honorary for one to put the neighbor's brand on his foals because next year the colt, or "slick," as he was known, without an iron would be anyone's property who may wish to claim him. There were still two or three acquaintances who made a business in estranged yearlings. You can imagine how tall I sat in the saddle next day when following the big work teams and wagons loaded with wood, me bringing three young horses to be broke to work and my very own yearling. You could not have touched me with a ten foot pole.

The Box R Cavvy

Ranch hands ran the Box R cavvy,
through the middle of town today;
On a rain-covered asphalt street,
in Wyoming, third week of May.

It shocked my subconscious being,
and my cowboy core came alive;
A dormant corner of my past,
awoke as I witnessed the drive.

Nothing appeared more out of place
than those sixty head of horses
Galloping down a blacktop luge,
a dichotomy of forces.

It was as if virtue and vice
were drawn from the very same well;
Horse shoes attacking the pavement,
like Heaven had spilled into Hell.

The contrast of muscle and steam
erased the harsh background of the truth;
Glass and iron melted away,
it re-lit a flame from my youth.

I watched outriders lead the herd,
their slickers forbidding the rain;
Streamlets dripping off of their hats,
and off each horse's tail and mane.

The melodic clop of horse hooves
drowned out the noises of the street;
The stress and pain of urban life
disappeared from under their feet.

Two worlds clashed in altercation
that echoed off the man-made walls;
The yin and yang of hide and steel;
rumbled down the alleys and halls.

Then like divine answer to prayer,
they came and went without warning;
As they vanished without fanfare,
my heart felt the pang of mourning.

But they left me feeling at peace,
knowing I'd soon be headed home
And did not have to stay behind
in the land of asphalt and chrome.

My damaged soul had been mended
by the healing vision of steeds;
Their beauty and power entwined,
fulfilling some primary needs.

Now the city seems more tranquil,
and perhaps a bit more savvy;
Since the day the concrete jungle,
played host to the Box R cavvy.

Shoeing Shetlands

One of Dad's fellow students at shoeing school

See, he is a pretty good sized feller,
his abdominal goiter's quite stellar,
So whenever he bends, his butt crack extends,
and his Wranglers drop into the cellar.

I haven't quite figured it out yet. Did Dad make us ride Shetland ponies when we were first learning because, a) they were short enough for us to saddle ourselves, or because, b) we were short enough to get under them and learn how to shoe. In either case, I believe the answer is a resounding *yes*. What a terrible thing to do to an aspiring young cowboy, saddle him with the most ornery and short-fused animal in the equine kingdom. Those biting, striking, and kicking little Lucifers are the bane of cowboy education and I witnessed one grab a little girl by the ponytail and shake her. Malicious little buggers. But there is one cowboy trait a Shetland can teach you faster than any other method; cussing! It is for sure and for certain, you have never really learned how to cuss until you have tried to shoe a Shetland. King and Prince were the royal steeds assigned to big brother Jim and me when we were but little shavers.

King was a squatty and fat dapple grey Shetland pony with the bad habit of laying down with you at any water crossing. Therefore, he was assigned to Jim. Jim was by no means a stubby legged little feller, but when he saddled up and mounted King, he looked like he was like riding a 500 gallon diesel fuel barrel while doing the Chinese splits. One of our favorite things to do on a hot summer day was to ride up past the rodeo grounds to an irrigation pond and run our horses through the cool water. Remember King's bad habit? He would lay down with Jim frequently and submerge them both, until one day Dad shared with Jim the solution. He told Jim all he had to do was when King went to lay down, jump off and sit on his head for a while, holding it underwater.

The plan was put into effect one day and the
splashing and flailing was intense. It looked like Jim
was riding a hairy egg-beater whipping up chocolate
milk, when all at once, King had enough and Jim
went flying. Better Olympic dives I have never seen
and I gave him a 5.9 for execution and difficulty of
dive, but the Czechoslovakian judge docked him for
his swimming suit.

Prince was more of a POA mix, rather than a straight
Shetland, but that didn't help his disposition any. He
was a stocky, sorrel tobiano paint, with a crested neck
and a mane that was always roached short, indicative
of the style back then. Dad was a wizard with the
roaching shears and had been known on occasion to
give Jim and me haircuts in the same style and
manner. But I digress. Prince was the rook of
runaway, duke of the ditch-and-dash, and the earl of
exit and escape. Man, that little pony was fast and he
could take the bit in his mouth and run. The key was
avoiding the runaway by implementing Dad's
instructions not to run back toward the house. The
method of putting the whoa to this runaway pony
varied, depending on where you were at the time. If
you couldn't get him shut down and you had a long
straight away, you let him run out. If you had a short
runway but plenty of open area around you, you
pulled his head to one side and made an airplane turn
until he quit. But, if you had neither, your best bet
was the *jerk and pray* method: jerk as hard and as
many times on the reins, as fast as you could, and
pray for a soft place to land, because there was a good
chance you both were going down. One particular
runaway, we had a ninety degree turn to make from

where we came, in order to get to the corrals. Prince
and I both knew this, but I was the only one who
knew it was a hard dirt road covered with loose
gravel. We took the corner at mach 3 and down we
went, but luckily I cushioned Prince's fall and he got
up and continued without me. I was scratched up
pretty good but no broken bones. And it wasn't all
bad; I received a steady flow of cards, candies, and
dandelions from the love of my life at the time,
Loretta. Runaways weren't Prince's only trick, he was
also a master of the scrap-off. He'd run you under
Mom's clothes line, a power pole support cable, or on
one occasion, the tree in our front yard, thus the
comminuted fractures of my right radius and ulna.

Not mentioned earlier, and not hardly worth the
mention, was Punky. See, Dad was frequently the
recipient of horses that no one else wanted. That
must be where I received my inclination to
unintentionally start the *Andy Nelson Rest Home for
Wayward, Crippled, or Otherwise Unwanted Horses.*
Sheesh! I guess I came by it honestly, because either
out of the softness of his heart, the softness of his
head, or because *free* was the right price, Dad rescued
many neglected horses. So, Punky came to live with
us. That poor little Shetland's feet had been neglected
for so long, his hooves curled forward like the
Munchkin's shoes in the Wizard of Oz. Armed with a
dehorning saw, Dad went to work with big brother
Jim and I as his surgical assistants. A person can't
eat an elephant like this in one setting, so after time,
Punky's feet were in better shape and big brother Jim
and I were now Punky's podiatrists.

Dad had plenty of experience with ponies of all
breeds and related one particular story that
showcases the tenacity of what he referred to as,
"the worthless little horses." In the '50s, Antelope
Island in the Great Salt Lake was stocked with a
dozen Shetland pony mares and a couple pony studs
because there was a bull market for them at the
time. The problem being, there was nobody around
to help them practice safe animal husbandry and
they were allowed to proliferate uncontrolled. When
the bottom finally dropped out of the pony market, a
hundred inbred feral ponies had choked out the
small island. Dad and a group of really good hands
were hired to round up the wild herd for transport
off the island.

There were a few good wrecks and many close calls
in the rounding up process, but my favorite story
involved a modern wrangler and a motorcycle. The
motorbike wrangler was pushing a small group of
ponies to the corral trap when a little black stud
turned back. The wrangler wheeled back, following
in hot pursuit. After a long sprint, the little stud got
winded and turned to do battle with the noisy
contraption chasing him. The stud pony grabbed the
handlebars of the motorcycle in his teeth and
violently shook the rider to the ground. Dad said he
often wondered how all survived with no real
catastrophes.

Harvey's Moon

Harvey's farrier skills are better than fair,
he's an equine podiatrist extraordinaire;
The best I've found, for miles around,
and is one that will take extra care

To be gentle with our ornery old donks,
patient with our green broke broncs;
Quiet and calm, never raises his palm,
and when entering the yard, never honks!

There's just one bad habit he carries,
I assume that's why he never marries;
When under a horse, his tush is the source,
of conversation and various inquiries.

See, he is a pretty good sized feller,
his abdominal goiter's quite stellar;
So whenever he bends, his butt crack extends,
and his Wranglers drop into the cellar.

I swear his permanent vertical smile
stretches for at least half of a mile;
He squats right there, with exposed derriere,
for an eternity... or at least quite a while!

At this point it is usually best,
to send the children away with the rest
of the weaker folks, and the older pokes
that can't stomach a farrier "half dressed."

It showers the bravest man with fright,
this awkward and ominous sight;
A sweaty crevasse, the crack of his (hiney),
a black hole that harbors no light.

Even the horses stare all bug eyed
at this spectacle there by their side;
Not sure what to think, they don't even blink,
they just gawk at his funny pale hide.

His dignity I'm tempted to purloin,
with his pants pulled down to his groin;
Every time that I casually walk by
I have this urge to put in a coin.

His modesty leaves much to be desired,
at an office job he'd surely be fired;
With a visible crease, all covered in grease,
but that's not the reason he was hired.

No matter what fashion crime he commits,
whether his Wranglers and his T-shirt fits;
He's by far the best farrier in the west,
and I hope and I pray he never quits.

Who cares if his butt resembles a prune,
he'll be back here next Tuesday at noon;
It ain't all that wrong, and like the old song,
I say go ahead, "Shine on, Harvey's Moon!"

4

The Big Crash

The young Nelson children left to right: Rex, Clara,
Rose (holding Jim), and Ruth at their homestead

Change comes at you in a hurry,
and it rends my heart asunder;
I've already seen the lightning,
...now I'm waiting on the thunder.

Written by James F. Walker Nelson

Before the big crash of the stock market and the
banks closing their doors I remember vividly riding
the derrick horse or a team on a so-called derrick
cart for $1.00 per 10 hour day and walking to the
cashier's window of the Farmer's Commercial and
proudly presenting my check for payment. I would
have had to have been in the 10 year-of-age bracket.
Then the crash came and the next year I received
$0.50 for a 10-hour day. There were many suicides in
the big cities but to us the most severe I can
remember of was a hair pulling.

When my mother would finally discard a pair of
worn out overalls of Dad's, she would always wash
and lay them outside the fence for another gent
down the road who would be by and very cautiously
look around before picking them up.

Alfalfa hay sold for about $5.00 to $6.00 per ton, but
people needing the hay usually didn't have the fiver
either. From April or May until the first curing, hay
was always scarce and every family had milk cows
and some horses. There was a fences pasture two to
three miles west of our place and three or four
families rented it and paid me to gather their milk
cows after milking time and drive them to pasture,
then deliver them back that evening. This was duck
soup for a young cowboy of 10 or 11 years of age and
$6.00 per month, too.

The Depression to me was a period of hard manual
work—plenty to eat—enjoyable times—and no

particular amount of money, but what the heck. My dad Gus would tell me of his childhood where there was no money and in return for labor one was issued script which was generally accepted at a dry goods store for the basic fundamentals. He would also tell of his father Anders hearing of a miracle stick called a match with which one could start a fire blaze by whipping it across your pant leg. A leg, a phenomenon which many today have not seen nor can they do, but the old timers of corn cob pipes of Bull Durham roll-your-own were masters of this art. One shrewd and miserly old gent conducted a survey as to whether Prince Albert or Bull Durham was the more economical. The result favored Prince Albert because it took fewer matches to keep it going.

The present-day cigs which will not go out are most obnoxious to a non-smoker, as well as to Smokey the Bear. Now, just how did we get on smoking when it was the Depression we were talking about? Well, okay, most all us young fellers had a snipe cache and while herding cattle or horses if our grounders ran out we could always go to cedar bark or dry horse manure. Whew!!! Either sure bit the tongue. In order to utilize the dry horse manure, we would use Dad's pipe. Dad would scrape the pipe, smell it and scrape some more.

Waiting on the Thunder

Our first child moved away last year,
she's grown now and all on her own;
We only see her on holidays,
or perhaps to co-sign a loan.

Change comes at you in a hurry,
and it rends my heart asunder;
I've already seen the lightning,
...now I'm waiting on the thunder.

Like waves of grass, life ebbs and flows,
and the only constant is change;
I choke down a lump in my throat,
as prosperity swallows the range.

My old cow dog is fourteen now,
how he lived this long, is a wonder;
I'm seeing more of the lightning now,
but I'm still waiting on the thunder.

Storm clouds of age gather o'er me,
arthritic aches go clean to the bone;
A couple horse wrecks still haunt me,
but the reaper has left me alone.

So I cherish bygone adventures,
and mind's memories I plunder;
I've sure seen lots of lightning and,
now I'm waiting on the thunder.

I've seen some good horses buried,
and bid farewell to trusted friends;
I deal with it best that I can,
and wait as my broken heart mends.

We're all holding on for dear life,
while the stock market goes under.
We've seen lightning like this before,
now we're waiting on the thunder.

As witness to a shrinking world,
we hold fast to our western roots.
We will never sell our saddles,
nor shame in our cowboy boots.

We ride the recession like a bronc,
and weather each Wall Street blunder.
We've a front row seat of the lightning,
and now we're waiting on the thunder.

What's in our hearts, keeps us going,
love of life, family and pards.
We forge onward through trials and fears,
and play whatever's in the cards.

Yet keep close to our traditions,
Never to divide asunder,
and it's okay, bring on the lightning,
I think we're ready for the thunder.

5

On the Road with Uncle Mode

Dad (in the truck bed) with Pat, Debbie, Doris, Jim
and an unknown feller holding up the shovel

*I'd just tossed a loop, when Duke shouted out,
"I've a soggy one on my twine";
A big brindle calf was jumping about,
like Duke with a trout on the line.*

"I'm gonna puke," is all I can remember blurting out as I lunged across Uncle Mode's lap, vaulting toward the passenger side door of the 1950s International Harvester pickup with the oxidized paint finish.

Uncle Mode was not really my uncle. I believe he was a distant cousin of my mother, but I loved that old cowboy as much as I did any uncle. I never knew his real given name and to this day all I know him by is Uncle Mode Hunter. He was not the best role model for a young boy who was still single-digit age, in fact, they call it "contributing to the delinquency of a minor," nowadays. As Uncle Mode would pull a Copenhagen can from the front pocket of his pearl-snapped denim shirt, I would inquire each and every time what it was. "Candy. Want some?" was always his response. Luckily, as a child I could never get past the nauseating smell long enough to give it a try.

I recall that the brandings out at the Hunter homestead were extra special. Not only did we get to wrestle the calves to our hearts' delight, but it was there we perfected our culinary skills in cooking the original fast food: calf fries. We didn't have the luxury of time, waiting for mom to clean, peel, bread, and fry those tender morsels; we had appetites to feed. Dad's shoeing forge, made from the guts of an old water heater and a hand crank blower, served as the branding fire and our cook stove. If you have a weak stomach, you may skip to the end of this paragraph. We would flop those pudgy pink amputations on the top of the forge and wait patiently for them to burst. Once they popped open, we were free to partake of the food of the Gods, indulging ourselves on fare known only to a select few.

You may now understand why my Mom had reservations when she agreed to let me accompany Dad and Uncle Mode on a horse shoeing safari down into northern Nevada. Now, Uncle Mode was not a farrier, but he had the distinction of being my Dad's copilot, navigator and bombardier (it was his responsibility to bring along the fifths of ammunition necessary for the bombing!). The agreement was, we would be gone all day Saturday and return late Saturday night, so I would be present, cleaned, and pressed for church Sunday morning. Upon Mom's consent, we were off like a plumb bubble in a whiskey stick.

The day was spent shoeing various horses in various locations with one strategic stop in Jackpot, Nevada for supplies. The use of the word supplies here refers not to shoeing supplies, but rather supplies consisting of adult beverages, a tube of salami, brick of cheese, crackers, pork rinds, and an Orange Crush. The sun was setting on a long day of hard work and getting home was high priority. Therefore, a shortcut through the high desert would be prudent. As Dad and Uncle Mode charted our course for home on a two-track road in which both tracks rarely went in the same direction, I slugged downed the Orange Crush and helped myself to the hors d'oeuvres. Now, it became clear in a very short time that alcohol and shortcuts do not mix... and before long, we were lost. I mean *lost*, as in, Amelia Earhart lost. More lost than Moses ever thought of being in forty years in the wilderness.

More lost than the feller who sings "Mariah" in *Paint Your Wagon*. Now that's lost!

We continued driving into a night that was darker than the inside of a cow. The glow of the IH high-beams barely pierced through the vacuum of blackness and the road, simply put, was not a road. We bounced, jiggled, shimmied, jarred, and catapulted across sage and greasewood until we found ourselves halted by an arroyo. Not just any arroyo, but the mother of all arroyos, an arroyote (meaning, one dang big wash). It might just as well have been the Grand Canyon because this wash was not navigable. We had come to the place where we would make camp for the night. There was no way to contact Mom and inform her of our predicament. All that could be done was bed down the best we could and wait for the sun to come up.

Dad and Uncle Mode had no problem falling asleep with the aid of liquid sleeping pills, but I on the other hand, had a problem. I was lost, homesick, scared and full of junk food that was well shaken, not stirred. I didn't want to wake up Uncle Mode but I could feel Mount Saint Salami about to erupt. I gave him one quick warning on my way across his lap and in a manner reminiscent of Herman Melville's novel, I blew.

We all put in a pretty rough night, the sun finally came up, and it was time to get un-lost. By the time we made it back home, it was late in the afternoon, Mom was hanging laundry out to dry and by the look in her eye, I figured Dad was next.

The Bar T Branding

It was branding time at the ol' Bar T,
and the boys were all gathered 'round;
Jasper had sent all the ropers with me,
while Zeke ran the crew on the ground.

The workers put on an awesome display,
the crew was a well-oiled machine;
Like crossing some bees, a Russian Ballet,
and a pile of ants on caffeine.

The ropers were crisp and true with their loops,
and the calves had nary a chance;
The muggers were strong and all of the troops
joined force in the front-line advance.

I'd just tossed a loop, when Duke shouted out,
"I've a soggy one on my twine";
A big brindle calf was jumping about,
like Duke with a trout on the line.

Then Duke dropped a coil, his dally slid through,
with thumb betwixt lasso and horn;
The calf took to air... and his thumb did too,
bursting like a piece of popcorn.

It tumbled mid air, with no where to go,
like a wiener seeking a bun,
Then flopped to the dirt and cow pies below,
and the crew set out on the run

To grab the darn thing before it got lost,
or claimed by a hungry stray pup;
They found it right where it was tossed,
when Zeke's Basset gathered it up.

All the men in the crowd yelled at the dog,
and he shifted into high gear;
Searching for cover behind a big log,
then beneath Zeke's truck at the rear.

Women, disgusted with the whole display,
coaxed the dog from under the truck;
The limb was retrieved, and without delay,
could be sewn back on with some luck.

The story ends well, with Duke and his thumb,
together, forever, for good;
It's still pretty stiff and partially numb,
and don't work a bit like it should.

But Duke brings it up, whenever he can,
and takes one more stab at poor Zeke;
He teases him how, a horse, dog and man,
had ended his calf roping streak.

He digs in some more, 'bout what might have been,
had it been ate by Zeke's Basset;
"Yep," Zeke will say, "I'd been full of chagrin,
just waiting for him to pass it."

6

Horse-Drawn Adventures

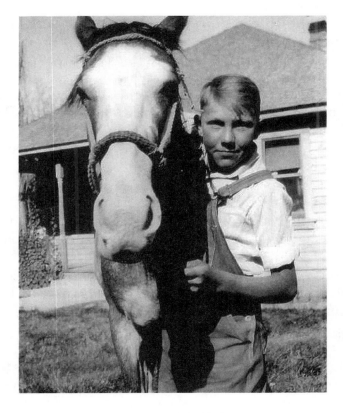

Dad age 13 with Calapucci

I hooked up the chain, and unhooked my brain,
slowly eased him into a walk;
He turned his head 'round, and looked at the ground,
and saw the pole chase him, in shock.

Written by James F. Walker Nelson

The Trapper Creek Ranch was one my dad and Jim Walker operated in a livestock operation which folded in the '20s. I must have been in the 7th grade of school that year. All fall and winter I babied the paint yearling Dad gave to me. I had taught my Brownie Bob dog to pull me in the little red wagon before I even started school. We had an old horse for the buggy and for riding and we came by a cart when the neighboring homestead was sold to us for taxes. Dad had parked our gasoline-consuming Model T Ford when the '29 crunch came, and he managed to save us and bought that neighboring forty.

The big owl-eyed bally horse that I rode when bringing in the "wild bunch" off the mountain seemed to me should be the proper engine to put in this cart. I harnessed him and put the blinders on his bridle (so he could not see behind him), put the cart in place, secured the shafts and tugs and climbed in. Clucked to him a bit, he did not move. Tapped him on the rump a bit, he looked around and saw the contraption behind him and that did it. The only thing I remember a-seeing for the next few minutes was a kind of a whirlwind mixed with dust and poop. When the fracas finally ceased the onliest thing intact was the owl-eyed bally horse. The cart and harness were strewn in pieces around the big yard. The cart seat had no back, so I was the first to go and the balance followed suit in very short and rapid order.

Ol' Bally, still wearing the blinder bridle, was in the far corner eye-balling his accomplishment. Dad showed up from somewhere. I now know that he knew there was going to be a tremendous show. I'm also sure he saw more than I did. He didn't need to survey the wreck 'cause I'm sure he watched it all from the stable window. What the heck, a dumb kid's gotta learn.

He asked why I didn't put the paint colt in instead of the bally horse. "Good gosh Dad, if the broke bally horse did this, the colt would really put up a fuss." "Try it anyway!" There was a way my father said things that needed no further comment. I gathered up the harness pieces to patch and I still had two wheels and an axle left of the cart and a very vivid recollection of the greatest performance witnessed of beast by man.

The painted stud colt had been christened Calapucci in honor of a sheepherder's dog with the same strawberry roan markings. He was not big nor quite old enough to ride but all winter I sneaked him an extra quart of oats every chance I had. In the spring when thinning beets I always came with my bibs full of sugar beet greens. As a matter of fact, I always had some kind of choice morsel whenever I went around the horse corral. He, being a two year old now—and with his extra rations—had put on exceptional growth. Dad allowed as to how I could start riding him out in the open. He had known for some time I had been sneaking rides with him. Somehow a boy cannot get away with anything. With the patched up harness and the rebuilt cart, I put Calapucci to the demolition test. To my amazement he moved off just as though he had been doing it for years. He had a

shuffling walk that developed into a pace and with a
little encouragement got nothing but faster. We were
the envy of some and the idol of others. Some old
grannies would cluck their tongues and wonder what
in tarnation Mrs. Nelson was thinking about to allow
my carryings on.

As I recall, that cart just did not seem to bode well. It
was the one that scattered Zelda and Kerma and me
in the sage the past Easter, when Maggie and Ardis
waved their aprons for us to stop. I must have been in
the 6th grade because it was before the Cal horse. We
had a good, gentle buggy horse and I had him in our
cart on Easter day. Two or three of the boys had
saddle horses but there were a couple of gals wanting
to Easter out on the east foothill. I don't recall about
it being a big banquet but at that time we always
appropriated eggs, bread, and butter. I harnessed our
old gentle horse to the cart. Now the cart seat was
really meant to accommodate one man, but two gals
and I fit on it a bit snugly. We went and rolled rocks
and ate boiled eggs and were coming home via Jerry
Stanger's east road. Here comes a brand new Durant
up the dusty sagebrush road. The old horse was
headed home on a big trot when out of the Durant
came two *big* women a-flopping their aprons to halt
the cart. There were no fences so the horse, cart, me,
and two girls took to the brush. Safety belts were
unheard of so it did not take but very few
sagebrushes to unload the occupants of the cart seat.
I could hear mama Elison screaming, "My daughter,
my dear daughter." About that time she picked up her
dear daughter, hugged and kissed on her and when
she discovered the dear darling was not hurt, she

uprooted a sagebrush and proceeded to hurt her. The big sister gathered the other girl up and I failed to witness anything else. The horse and cart were way down the road and there was a lateral canal which I cleared in two jumps. Big Maggie offered me a ride home, but even at that tender age, I was smart enough to say no thanks.

Clyde the Destroyer

I see some birdies, all kinds of purties,
and shooting stars about my head;
I've way too much pain, this side of my brain,
for me to be peacefully dead.

I sure met my match, there in the weed patch,
an eighteen-hand Belgian warrior;
A one-ton galoot, a feather-hoofed brute,
my work horse, "Clyde the Destroyer."

I had this wise thought, that I really ought
to teach him to pull logs and stumps;
He's strong and limber, and can snake timber,
over dead fall, scrub brush and bumps.

He's sure enough stout, and there is no doubt,
he could pull Hell out of its hole;
We'd begin real slow, with lumber in tow
and start with an old power pole.

I hooked up the chain, and unhooked my brain,
slowly eased him into a walk;
He turned his head 'round, and looked at the ground,
and saw the pole chase him, in shock.

The faster he strode, the faster it rode,
stalking him like wolves in the night;
He tried to ditch it, but couldn't pitch it.
so stepped up his runaway flight.

With my lines in hand, I covered the land,
like a water skier in tow;
My feet touched the ground, 'bout every third bound,
I knew I was running too slow.

Then Clyde ran faster, than I could master,
I fumbled, then stumbled and cursed;
I toppled and spun, and flat come undone,
like a moth in a micro burst.

I heard my neck crack, each joint in my back,
wobbled like a grade schooler's top;
I prayed that the pole, would miss me in whole,
and that Clyde would finally stop.

My vision was blurred, and a dust storm stirred,
as ol' Clyde hastened his retreat;
I watched him run by, with my one good eye,
dragging the pole across my feet.

He ran for the barn, and safety from harm,
but snagged the pole on the hay rake;
He tore through the tugs, like a train on drugs,
leaving piles of junk in his wake.

I gathered my thoughts, and felt the head knots,
raising like grandma's homemade rolls;
I'd scream if I could, to heck with the wood,
I think I'll just buy posts and poles.

My wife left this thought, "That surely was not
the smartest thing you ever did;
It's easy to cure, ignorance for sure,
but there's just no fixing 'stupid'!"

Dad ready for a parade in the late '50s or early '60s

7

Full Nelson Shoeing

Big brother Jim (right) and I in action

Photo by Stuart Johnson

With our tools in hand, we travel the land,
poor bare-footed foals we are pursuing;
Have forge to go, smell like DMSO,
we're the men of the Full Nelson Shoeing!

As farriers, we may not be the brightest bunch in general, but we are friendly. Being friendly is a prerequisite to shoeing. Believe it or not, one has to be a people-person to shoe horses. Oh sure, it is the horse you are working on, but it is his owner who is waiting patiently to jump in the middle of you like a crow waiting to land on a fresh road kill. Whether you are shoeing a performance horse, a working horse, or a close member of the family, the owners see it as if this animal's fate is resting in your hands. One slip of the tongue or unkind word and you incur the wrath of the owner as their entire world comes crashing down around you. It is your fault the bulls do not get put in with the cows on time, it is your fault the filly takes last place in the futurity, it is your fault that Penelope doesn't break 19 seconds in the barrel race, it is your fault the heeler missed his loop, it is your fault the big one got away, it is your fault Killer dumped the mother-in-law *(the farrier is not always chastised for this one)*, and it is your fault his wife asked him for a divorce.

Proper shoeing etiquette includes showing up on time, *on the right day*, fielding any and all questions hurled in your direction by the owner, and providing a little comic relief in a tense situation. You are the owner's friend, confidante, therapist, financial advisor, weather man, market reporter, vet tech, ag extension officer, and horse whisperer... you are their farrier, trusted and revered throughout the land. It is with this knowledge in hand, I share with you the account of how big brother Jim and I were christened, *"Full Nelson Shoeing."*

We worked in an efficient assembly line manner that even John Henry Ford would be proud of. I jerked the shoes and prepared the hoof as big brother Jim came in behind shaping and nailing the shoes on, then I followed up with the clinching, this all being done in a round-robin fashion. We could fly through the horses this way and on one particular occasion whipped out twenty dude horses in one visit to the DC Bar ranch.

The Full Nelson Shoeing moniker came to life after a lady horse owner called Jim to shoe her young filly. I accompanied Jim to the appropriate place where she was anxiously waiting with a three- or four-year-old filly. No one had ever shod this filly before but it was evident she had her feet played with a few times. As I began to address the on-side front hoof, I heard big brother Jim's mischievous voice declare, "Brace yourself little brother, I'm going to try something." Holy cow, what was he going to do that I needed to brace myself for? I envisioned many things, but what he ended up doing surprised even me. While I was in the air with the on-side front, Jim stealthily eased the off-side hind off the ground and began to do a little knife work on the sole. The horse stood still! So, we carried on. Jim nipped and rasped the hind and I completed the preparation for shoeing of the front. This whole time, the owner of the horse was agog, nay, aghast at the vision she beheld. Not sure whether to cheer, scream, or faint, she watched as Jim and I worked in a very matter-of-fact manner and her precious little filly patiently let us. I've always felt the reason the horse didn't explode was because she was confused, she didn't know whether to bite me or kick Jim. Nonetheless, the filly had new

shoes and big brother Jim and I had a new story to
tell that came with a new dba (doing business as)
name, *Full Nelson Shoeing*.

Full Nelson Shoeing

We are the guys that your mothers despise,
they don't care for the things we're doing;
We just shoe horses, have no resources
we're the men of the Full Nelson Shoeing!

With our tools in hand, we travel the land,
poor bare-footed foals we are pursuing;
Have forge to go, smell like DMSO,
we're the men of the Full Nelson Shoeing!

Either donk or steed, we got what you need,
we'll shoe you anything that ain't mooing;
Our spines are wrecked, and we're a bit rednecked,
we're the men of the Full Nelson Shoeing!

The shoers are twice, and so is the price,
and there's no sense sitting there stewing;
Want it today? Shoulda called yesterday,
we're the men of the Full Nelson Shoeing!

And the price expands, with certain demands,
like when Buttercup needs a shampooing;
We don't do fluff, we neither wax nor buff,
we're the men of the Full Nelson Shoeing!

Bad habits may abide, where we reside,
but neither of us indulge in chewing;
We may impart, an occasional... belch,
we're the men of the Full Nelson Shoeing!

Our bellies may sag, and our butts may drag,
but you'll never hear us boo-hooing;
Scenes of fresh Krispy Kremes dance in our dreams,
we're the men of the Full Nelson Shoeing!

Then it's Mountain Dew, for me and for you,
it's them with the deep pockets we're wooing;
Some show horses here, there's a race track near,
for the men of the Full Nelson Shoeing!

Sweaty and dirty, never look purty,
a good batch of body odor brewing;
The smell we built, could make a flower wilt,
we're the men of the Full Nelson Shoeing!

There's so many scabs, on my arms and abs,
looks like I have received some tattooing;
Your horses are fine, this blood is all mine,
and from the men of the Full Nelson Shoeing!

We're proud farriers, not purse carriers,
we shoe horses for riding not gluing;
Rugged and tuff, we just can't get enough,
we're the men of the Full Nelson Shoeing!

If your horses kick, or strike, bite or lick,
here's some tips to avoid someone suing;
Just go to the mall, and don't *even* call,
the men of the Full Nelson Shoeing!

Cowboy Etiquette

Dad doing a little cooking on his camp stove

*She raked me back and forth across the coals
like a helpless, roasting wiener;
And she said my manner was appalling,
not to mention my demeanor.*

Written by James F. Walker Nelson

Dear Crabby,
When my husband comes in from the corrals, he
washes his boots in the toilet. He puts in one foot
and scrubs it until it comes clean, then pulls the
chain to get clean water. Then he washes the other
boot. Is this proper etiquette for a cowboy?
Signed, Flushed with Anger

Dear Flushed,
There are some things a cowboy was never meant to
use. Indoor plumbing is one of them. The other
things that a cowboy was never meant to use are: a
shovel, a calculator, a pipe wrench, food stamps, a
tractor, a squeeze chute, a grease gun, and a lawyer.
Yours in etiquette, Crabby

U

Dear Crabby,
I am an old broken down cowboy who lives in a line
shack. A fellow cowboy friend of mine is having a
shower. Well, actually, he is taking one. Do I need to
send a gift for this occasion? It is a first for both of
us.
Love, Stinky

Dear Stinky,
A new pair of white long-handled underwear would
be appropriate.
Signed, Crabby

Dear Ann Slanders,
I just started dating cowboys. It has been a new
experience to say the least. I was wondering... are
dumb cowboys as sexy as the other kind?
Yours truly, Puzzled

Dear Puzzled,
What other kind?
As always, Ann Slanders

Dear Emily Compost,
I am a lonely 80-year-old rancher. I own 40,000 acres
and have a million dollars in the bank. I have fallen
madly in love with a beautiful 23-year-old blonde.
My health is far from robust. Do you think I would
have a better chance of marrying the blonde if I told
her I was 60?
Sincerely, Ready but not able

Dear Ready,
I think you would have a better chance if you told
the beautiful blonde that you were 95 years old.
Don't forget to mention your health. By the way, I'd
love to meet you.
Singularly yours, Emily xoxoxox

        ♡

Dear Ann Slanders,
I am a lonely 30-year-old cow puncher and I can't
seem to find the right girl. The last girl I took out
was really strange. She tied me up in chains and did
strange things to me. I broke my arm in three places.
Signed, Desperate and confused

Dear Desperate,
Stay out of these places. Stop waiting for the right
girl. Just do your best with the wrong one.
Remember, don't pick your teeth with your
castrating knife, nobody'll kiss a cowboy on the first
date if he's chewing tobacco, scratch where it itches,
never eat more than you can lift, and never pass gas
before your girlfriend... her turn first.
Best regards, Ann Slanders

Sensitivity Training

My sister informed me I was tactless,
she was tired of my complaining;
Then she said I was in urgent need of
some sensitivity training.

She raked me back and forth across the coals
like a helpless, roasting wiener;
And she said my manner was appalling,
not to mention my demeanor.

I said there wasn't a blessed thing wrong
with my demeanor you can bet;
The more people tend to irritate me,
"Da meaner and meaner" I get.

She said I had perfectly proved her point,
and she commenced to fill my ear;
With etiquette, regulations, and rules,
dispensing all manner of fear.

I knew nothing of these bylaws,
or why they were being enforced;
Double dipping a chip is forbidden,
and belching may get you divorced.

The one-finger nose-blow is disgusting,
scratching is offensive and rude;
You must take off your hat for a photo,
but hat-head is equally crude.

You can't go swimming in your undershorts,
and Wranglers are not formal wear;
You are not supposed to use a washcloth,
for combing and parting your hair.

Don't sit in your truck and honk for your wife,
or make her ride the horse that bucks;
Do not clean your fingernails during lunch,
and don't be shooting at park ducks.

Take your spurs off at the dinner table,
and don't cuss for any reason;
And do not take a shot at the tourists,
even if it's "tourist season."

You can't swim in the city aquifer,
it's crass to pinch your neighbor's wife;
I am just about to go plum crazy,
with these important rules of life.

So I told my sister I'd had enough,
of all this etiquette and such;
People will have to take me as I am,
a poke that don't get to town much.

9

Farrier School

The mighty farrier Dylan

May your anvil be tempered, your hammers be tight,
and your tools not go as loaners;
May your horses stand quiet, with never a bite,
I wish the same for their owners.

Big brother Jim and I have sons who are quick
becoming the heirs-apparent to the Nelson horse
shoeing dynasty. Well, *dynasty* may be a bit too
flattering, so we'll just refer to it as the next
generation of farriers. Dad taught Jim and I how to
shoe horses, but a feller truly becomes a farrier by
lots of sweat-soaked t-shirts. Whether you intend to
make a living shoeing horses or not, knowing how to
put on a set of shoes is an important trade to have if
one owns horses. Therefore, teaching the trade to my
boys has been a priority for me.

I owned a leggy, bay Three Bars mare named Gypsy
that was one of the best teachers of little cowboys I
ever had. She was quiet, calm and patient... except
when it came to shoeing. She and I had a ritual we
went through every spring and I am not
exaggerating, I mean *every* spring; this was more
dependable than the atomic clock in Greenwich. I
believe she dreamed about it all winter and with
great anticipation, honestly looked forward to it. The
exchange would take place as I began putting shoes
on my horses for the new season and commenced
annually in the following manner. I would tie Gypsy
to the hitching post inside the dirt floor barn and
begin trimming the on-side front. Because of either
habit or heredity, this is the hoof I always start with
and then I methodically move in a counter-clockwise
direction until all four on the floor have been shod.
With the on-side front uneventfully shod, I would
then move to the on-side hind, signaling for the circus
to begin. Because she was substantially taller than I,
Gypsy would quickly pull her hind leg away from me
and recoil it back in my direction with a love tap. I

call it a love tap instead of a kick because it was a
subtle movement designed more to say, "Mine... not
yours," rather than, "I'm going to kick your liver
loose!"

One particular day my son Dylan (probably about six
or seven years old at the time) was assisting me as
the tool pusher. He would hand over the proper tool
as I requested it. Gypsy was fully cocked and ready to
challenge my authority, but I was laying in wait for
her this time. I knew what was coming so I took an
extra tough constrictor grip on her leg as I laid it in
my lap and tucked her hock underneath my armpit...
when she jerked this time, I would be ready. She fired
and I held fast. Ha! She was unsuccessful in her
attempt... but I took just a little too much time
savoring my victory and let her hock slip out from
under my armpit and she fired again, this time
putting the onion to it. It must have surprised her
when her leg came free because with as much force as
it came loose, it came screaming back in my direction
and locked on target with my left butt cheek. It
sounded worse than it felt, kinda like the sound a zip-
lock bag full of vegetable soup makes when dropped
out of a dorm room window (don't ask how I know
that sound). Physics dictates that when a body in
motion meets an immovable object, force is converted
into energy and that energy must go somewhere or
dissipate... well, that energy translated into a
tumbling farrier. I pin-wheeled across the dirt floor,
flailing my arms like a 4-H county fair clogging team
in an effort to stay on my feet and salvage my ego. I
eventually gave up the fight to right my ship and not-
so-gracefully plowed a furrow in the barn floor with

my face. My surroundings appeared almost like in a
dream, things were hazy. I could hear a voice but
could not see anyone. The heavenly vision I was
experiencing wasn't because my bell was rung or that
I was on a precipice looking to the other side. It was
because I stirred up one heckuva dust storm inside
the barn with my dance number and the voice I heard
was Dylan's. He wasn't terribly worried about the
patriarch of his family being hurt, he just wanted to
make sure he wasn't destined for the same fate. He
stood defiantly over the top of me and proclaimed,
"See Dad, that's why I want to be a fireman and not a
horse shoer." Smart boy.

A Farrier's Toast

May your anvil be tempered, your hammers be tight,
and your tools not go as loaners;
May your horses stand quiet, with never a bite,
I wish the same for their owners.

May your trainers be kind, and they never reprove,
at home and to far distant lands;
May you ever be able, and always remove,
that nasty thrush smell from your hands.

May your nails be "five city," your shoes be all "oughts,"
with nail holes that never forge closed;
May joy fill your psyche, and garner your thoughts,
and your tush be seldom exposed.

May the mosquitoes not bother, and horse flies pass,
and joys never cease to wonder;
May your horses not colic, and never pass gas,
least while you're standing there under.

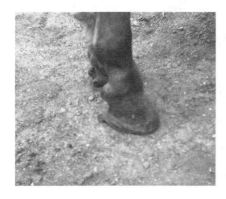

Two of Dad's friends at shoeing school 1957,
Dean Pickrel top and Ronald Schaefer bottom

10

Cattle Battles

Dad working a young one at the Wine Cup ranch

Then away she went, startled and intent
on dragging John along in tow;
The knot pulled tighter, as John would fight her,
and faster the heifer would go.

Written by James F. Walker Nelson

Northwest of town at a prominent farming/ranching operation, a young, self-taught cowboy vet attempted a disastrous cow-calf extraction. The big cow had just begun her labor when the ambitious young fellow thought she needed help. His wife focused the light from the van as he readied his calf pulling gear. Over the one foot which protruded he slipped a loop and snugged it up. Then after fashioning another loop over his wrist, he put that hand inside exploring for the other foot. The cow, not being really ready for the big push, decided to change maternity wards, the beginning of one of the greater Wild West Shows. She jumped up and took off looking for a new bed to have her baby. Well, there the tall, gangly six-foot-four-inch puller became the pullee. The lights from the van cast grotesque shadows as the cow really spooked. The pullee was led along by great strides 'til he ran out of gas. Now he became the dragee. The old bally cow, becoming enraged, tried kicking him off, then whirling and circling, tried to horn him off. The little woman was following all this time, trying to keep him in the headlights and avoiding the rest of the now-spooked herd. The dragee, near to passing out, somehow managed to get the noose off the calf. His wife helped him in the van and took him to the emergency room. He was hospitalized with a broken collar bone, a fractured wrist, and severely injured dignity. The mama cow found a new maternity ward and gave birth to her baby.

I was relating this bit of info to a cow rancher friend and he had to tell me of an incident involving the head end. The Doc vet was at the ranch to draw blood for the dreaded "Bangs" test. At that time the sample was taken from the neck. The cows were trapped in a squeeze chute and a helper with a pair of nose tongs would pull the cow's head around so Doc could draw a sample. The tongs had a nylon rope tied to them in order to get a better leverage. The gent using the tongs figured if he tied the rope around his waist he could pull more, and besides that, the tongs would always be with him. This all worked very well until the chap operating the gate-release figured there could be quite a show if the release slipped a little soon. Sure now, as hell is a-fire, it was a show. The old cow, already on the fight, came a charging out of the gate. There was no way the tongs man could turn her loose. The rope held fast and so did the tongs. He was snotted on, pawed on, kicked and messed on, all the way across the corral. When the commotion hit the fence on the other side the tongs came loose but the lad came up with the rope around his middle and the tongs securely tied to the end. The grand finale of another action packed moment of the Wild West.

A Cow's Tail Tale

The winters grow old, and stay very cold,
on the Green where John runs his cows;
When one turned up sick, he brought her in quick,
to doctor as spare time allows.

As the days passed on, she was nursed by John,
and she regained her health and all;
As she convalesced, her tail acquiesced,
to a cantaloupe-sized ice ball.

It swung when she'd walk, was hard as a rock,
and weighed about twenty-plus pounds;
She began to yearn, for a quick return,
to the cows out on the feed grounds.

So one sunny day, as she slept away,
John had a great epiphany;
He'd give it a kick, just one real good lick,
and bust the cow's pendulum free.

He lined up his strike, kinda field-goal like,
and a football kick was dispatched;
It never shattered, instead it battered,
against the barn wall still attached.

The ice-ball bounced back, and took up the slack,
stuck to the tail of the bovine;
John shortly found, it looped right around
his leg and tied in a bowline.

Then away she went, startled and intent
on dragging John along in tow;
The knot pulled tighter, as John would fight her,
and faster the heifer would go.

They made two loops now, both John and the cow,
in the hard cow-pie studded pen;
She drug him with ire, like calf to the fire,
and walloped him time and again.

She made a detour, through frozen manure,
still kicking at him with her hocks;
But John made the ride, though hard as she tried,
to scrape him off on the salt box.

As the box collapsed, John's pea-brain synapsed,
and he recalled his pocket-knife;
He then dug it out, and turned it about,
in an attempt to save his life.

When in between jumps, over troughs and bumps,
John shot up like a breaching whale;
He lunged at her rear, and swung without fear,
amputating the heifer's tail.

Then he lay there bruised, bleeding and contused,
as the cow continued irate;
He surveyed his pains, cut off the remains,
and nailed it to the lodge-pole gate.

Like a prize it hung, on the gate's top rung,
the ice-ball, appendage, and all;
And there it would stay, for many a day,
like a frozen bell-clapper ball.

Now, folks that go out, still inquire about,
ruminant remnants on a nail;
And John will retort, a yarn of some sort,
starting with, "Therein, hangs a tale."

11

Country Education

My oldest, Sadie, and my youngest, Abby in 1997,
on Sadie's little paint mare, Pepsi

I hope my children learned from me,
and will not suffer my mistakes;
I pray they keep this cowboy way,
always, through whatever it takes.

I have come to the stark realization that we as
parents are not the only people doing the teaching in
our households. Never a day goes by when our
children don't chime in with a bit of philosophy that
would even make Freud seek a turn on the couch.
There is never a dull moment in our house.

For instance, our youngest son Will taught me that
an optimist thinks that this is the best possible
world and a pessimist fears that is true. Will is ever
the optimist and has been since he was a baby. Will
was no older than three when one summer day he
and I were driving to town on our dirt road and
happened upon a road kill porcupine. Now, road kill
is not an occasional happening on our county road;
I'd say it's more the norm than the exception, but
this day was particularly gruesome. The lumbering
ol' porky-bear met his demise at the hand of a
speeding pick-up truck and had laid there in the
middle of the road in the hot summer sun for a
couple of days. Keep in mind a porcupine is a
formidable adversary either dead or alive, and any
person in his or her right mind would drive around
the corpse rather than stop to move it. A dead
porcupine is not like a gopher that gets run over so
many times and is baked hard and flat enough to
pick up and chuck like a Frisbee, or like a deer that
you can grab by what's left of a leg and drag into the
barrow-pit where crows, magpies, and the occasional
bald eagle make it into a neighborhood "Road-kill
Grill." So there he lay. The heat, micro-organisms,
and fermentation worked their wonders on the large,
uncoordinated rodent until he looked like a steroid-
laden barrel cactus with legs. I mean, he was

distended! If you would have pulled out a quill he would have rocketed off like a full, unknotted balloon. It was a grotesque vision but Will being the optimist, let out a sigh, as little kids do, and blurted out, "Aw, cute!" Always finding the silver-lining, making the lemonade, and waiting for the rainbow— our son will do fine in this world.

The contrast to Will's peaches-and-ice cream-existence is our youngest daughter Abby's realism. Abby is matter-of-fact and calls it as she sees it. Trying to sugarcoat things for Abby is an insult to her intelligence. At an early age, Abby had the unique ability to differentiate the genders of animals... a great talent, yes... but often embarrassing for those traveling with her. During an Old West Days parade in Valentine, Nebraska, the adolescent Abby stopped in front of a western-wear store where a life-size, rearing statue of a horse adorned the front of the building. With many parade-goers around she proclaimed, "See Dad, that one is a stallion," pointing up at the nether-regions of the statue, following her statement up with, "Yep, you can tell by the..." when she was instantly interrupted by her mother. Not satisfied that we all knew what she meant, she started in again, "I mean, it's not a gelding because he still has his...", as a volley of affirmations rang out through downtown Valentine. Abby is a stickler for anatomical correctness and on one her birthdays received a new Breyer model horse. Now, Breyer horses are well known for their accuracy in portraying different breeds, as well as genders, of horses. The particular model horse Abby was given was a beautiful paint gelding. Abby was thrilled with the present but disappointed with the gender and proceeded take out her pocket knife and whittle off the toy horse's manhood because she wanted a mare, not a gelding. Whew, when she grows up and starts a family of her own, let's hope she is satisfied with the gender of her first born!

These first two personalities mentioned have nothing on their older sister, Sadie. Sadie's personality is a cross between Will's optimism and Abby's realism, with a generous dose of naivety thrown in the mix. Either by accident or misfortune, I found myself in the foal business. I had a handful of brood mares around and foals were hitting the ground periodically. Sadie being the oldest, but still in single-digit age, was my right-hand man by default. She helped me with the new mamas and babies whether I needed the help or not. I knew that inevitably the question of where the babies came from would come up. It did... and I panicked! Never having been confronted with such a question before, I skipped the gear that engages my brain and went straight to the gear that engages my mouth and I offered to take Sadie along on the next trip to the stud. Now, the ol' stud was a handsome devil, a palomino paint named "Spud," and this was the perfect opportunity to take Sadie's little sorrel paint mare to be serviced. I did my best to explain everything before we arrived to have the mare bred. Well, we watched the stud "breed," (that was the term I used to explain the process to my daughter) the mare and there were no more questions afterward. That is how the babies got in there.

Satisfied with the whole ordeal, we headed home with the little paint mare and I was feeling pretty good about myself. I handled that situation quite well all by myself and I had to brag a little to the missus about my conquest. But my pride turned to humility in a hurry during supper that night. As we all sat around the table discussing the day's events, Sadie turned to me and with a straight face asked me, "Dad, when are you going to breed Mom?" I was mid-stream in a glass of Chateaux Moo when she dropped that lead balloon and I expectorated what I could out of my mouth. The rest came out my nose, like a grade-schooler laughing at an off-color joke in the school cafeteria. Now, she only wanted a younger sibling and she had just learned where babies come from, so it was a logical question in her mind. My wife just about swallowed her tongue in an involuntary conniption fit and snapped back at her, "Sadie, animals breed, humans conceive." She then shot me a look that could have burned a hole in the bottom of the space shuttle. The debriefing immediately began and damage control was skillfully executed by my wife, while I quietly finished what was on my plate and slipped out the back door en route to the barn. I cleaned stalls, oiled tack, and reset shoes on a couple horses until I came to the conclusion I would eventually have to go back in the house. Give my dear wife her due; she took it easy on me and we both just thanked our lucky stars this episode happened at our supper table and not at the local church picnic.

The Best Things in Life

I saw an old friend yesterday,
a pard I had not seen in years;
We talked about the good old days,
and laughed until we were in tears.

Reminisced our favorite horses,
and remembered some dandy wrecks
in the days when we used to ride,
with wild rags tied around our necks.

Then we talked about a few friends
who had been gone for not too long;
When his eyes welled up into tears,
and I asked if something was wrong.

He said, "Do you ever suppose,
folks will miss us after we're dead?"
His question stabbed me in the heart,
and echoed inside of my head.

Well, he sure got me to thinking,
and I haven't slept much since then;
"Did my life make a difference?"
this phrase haunts me time and again.

But I did teach my kids to ride,
taught them 'bout honesty and truth;
Instilled in them a sense of pride,
to help them along through their youth.

I taught the value of their word,
and a handshake to seal a deal;
To kill enemies with kindness,
and that verbal wounds may not heal.

They learned most their habits from me,
I can't say that's always been good;
But we sure worked hard together,
and played hard each chance that we could.

I hope my children learned from me,
and will not suffer my mistakes;
I pray they keep this cowboy way,
always, through whatever it takes.

Because cowboys aren't always judged
simply by how they rope or ride;
They are most often measured by
their integrity deep inside.

So, deep within I leave my mark,
and to my kids I leave this lore;
The best things in life are not *things*,
And do not come out of a store.

12

Bucking Off

Dad on the business end of the rope at a branding in
the Basin east of Oakley

*Why do I keep her? She pounds me each time,
I swing a leg and get on her;
She cost way too much, and ain't worth a dime,
each ride I think I'm a goner.*

Written by James F. Walker Nelson

I have rubbed elbows with men from every walk of life. One gets them all in an outfitter's lodge and hunting camps, but it has been in the cow camps where spontaneous humor crops out. The cowboy with humor is the one who shortens the long hours and miles on a cattle drive. This incident happened about the fifth day out of a seven-day cattle drive to spring range. Trucking at that time was unheard of. A bob-tail truck for supplies was a recent luxury. A big cow dropped a calf in the middle of the afternoon. The calf was loaded in the "cowmissary" truck and that evening we camped in a little sheltered basin with good grass, sagebrush, and juniper trees. I was riding a big 17-hand horse well capable of handling the 1,200 pound cow I was about to catch. A hard and fast loop over the horn, I roped the cow in order to suckle the calf. I rode up and dallied short and the cantankerous old horse exploded. I dropped the dallies and tried to straighten the bucking bronc out, and by then the cow came to an end of her rope. She hit broadside straight away. I flew through the air down the rope and luckily landed on my feet. Witty cowboys came riding up, "Don't dog her Jim, give me a chance to heel her!" The saddle turned completely over with the lariat between the horse's legs and had the mother cow wound around a juniper tree. The old cow nearly choked to death. A young cowboy with a halter came riding up. I haltered the cow and tied her to the tree, uncinched my saddle from the bronc and all three (cow, horse, and me) were trying to get our air. An old, but active cowboy came riding up, surveyed the situation and said, "The greatest show I ever witnessed on God's little acres."

That evening after a scrumptious supper, the crew was sitting around a sagebrush fire (rolling Bull Durham and sipping coffee) recounting the day's event the berrwhiskered "Olly" asked a young feller what he would have done in a situation of that sort. The young feller said, "I'd have spurred the ol' hoss." To which Olly replied, "Why sonny, there ain't enough bob wire in Texas to even wire your pants to the saddle of that ol' hoss."

The Worst One to Buck

She chatters my teeth, and rattles my bones,
and she is the worst one to buck;
She squeals like a pig, she snorts and she moans,
and shimmies like an old feed truck.

She beats on my kidneys, bruises my spleen,
and is cantankerous as heck;
Runs away at will, she's ornery and mean,
and thrills in whiplashing my neck.

Why do I keep her? She pounds me each time,
I swing a leg and get on her;
She cost way too much, and ain't worth a dime,
each ride I think I'm a goner.

She just takes her head, goes as she pleases,
no matter what cue I give her;
She breaks plum in two, jumps, kicks and wheezes,
jarring my tonsils and liver.

I tell her back up, she plows straight ahead,
runs bucking and stirring up dust;
She spews out exhaust, and revels instead,
in flaunting her growing distrust.

With all her bad habits, noises and smells,
she plain torques me off every day;
If I didn't need her, to clean my corrals,
I'd give that darn skid steer away.

13

The Mystery Behind Shoeing Fees

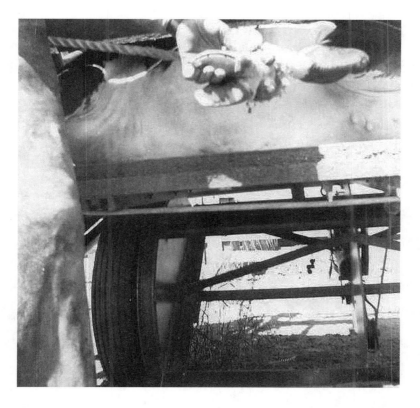

Dad working on a cow at shoeing school, circa 1957

*Our cowboy rigs sink clear to the axles,
and cows disappear in the chutes;
As the mud creates just enough suction
to pull off your rubber muck boots.*

"That will be $75.00 sir," are the most common words spoken by a farrier... and the most common response from the new horse owner not accustomed to the high cost of equine upkeep is, "Are you kidding me, that's robbery!" Perhaps, but that is the charge and the price will continue to rise the more the owner argues. For ease of understanding the farrier's price schedule, let me share with you a sample bill from the Full Nelson Shoeing corporation, with world headquarters in Pinedale, Wyoming. To the farriers who are reading this book, feel free to adopt this schedule as your own at no extra cost.

Full Nelson Shoeing form another angle

Photo by Stuart Johnson

Shoeing Fees Unbundled

Full Nelson Shoeing
Pinedale, WY
Try our easy payment policy;
100% down, no interest, no payments.

Order #:	Dept:	Date:

Name:
Address:
City, State, Zip:

Sold by: *Me*	Cash: *Yes*	On Acct: *No*	Charge: *No*	COD: *Hell No*	MDSE Rtd:?	Paid Out: *Now*

Quantity	Description	Price	Total
1	Basic Shoeing	$50.00	$50.00
4	Rim Shoes	$2.50	$10.00
32	#5 City Head Nails	$0.10	$3.20
2	Wasted Fuel from Poor Directions	$10.00	$20.00
1	Catching Your Horse Fee	$20.00	$20.00
1	"I trimmed him myself" Fee	$40.00	$40.00
1	Jerked a Nail Through My Hand Fee	$20.00	$20.00
1	Tetanus Booster + Stitches	$175.00	$175.00

572	Flurries of Bad Words	$0.01	$5.72
5	"Don't hurt him" Fee	$5.00	$25.00
1	"Are you sure you're doing it right" Fee	$100.00	$100.00
1	Pints of My Blood, Not His	$2.37	$2.37
7	Free Veterinary Advice	−$1.00	−$7.00
15	Training Tips	$2.00	$30.00
2	Psychiatric Evaluations (Human)	$20.00	$40.00
1	911 Call	Free	Free
1	911 Cancellation	$100.00	$100.00
	Grand Total		$607.29

Mud Season

Whoever said nothing can be certain,
only death and taxes are sure;
Never spent a spring time in Wyoming,
and never had mud to endure.

Our extra season comes after winter,
as sure as cows chewing their cud;
And before we can dive into summer,
we battle the infernal mud.

We spend the whole winter praying for snow,
and we praise every little flake;
Then we put the "Whoa Nellie" on praying,
when the drifts melt into a lake.

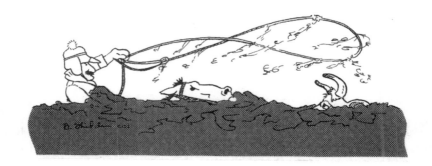

We wallow, we sludge, we spin, and we sink,
then we curse every bog and hole;
We struggle, we trudge, we trip, and we toil,
as we root and dig like a mole.

Our cowboy rigs sink clear to the axles,
and cows disappear in the chutes;
As the mud creates just enough suction
to pull off your rubber muck boots.

We gripe and we moan through the whole ordeal,
but we really shouldn't complain;
It won't be long until we are whining,
because we're in need of some rain!

14

Brownie Bob and Trapping

Dad as a youngster with a new basketball

*I try to be the kind that would
help others out of a jam;
And I hope I can be just half
the man my dog thinks I am.*

Written by James F. Walker Nelson

I still had my good "Brownie" dog, the one that got
his tail caught in the gears of the pump jack. The
cogs caught the end of his tail and just started
winding and grinding him in. By the time I got the
motor shut off he was in the gears up to his butt.
After that his name was "Brownie Bob."

This same dog caught me a skunk. We were walking
across the head ditch of the field and Brownie dove
in a currant patch. He came out with a young skunk
just a-literally shaking the scent out of him. I was
very proud of them both. I found a forked stick and
carefully balanced my prize on it and headed for the
house. To this day, I don't know how Mother knew
we were coming. We made it through the stake yard
and half way across the corral, didn't even make it to
the house yard gate before being whoa'd up. From a
safe distance Mom had me disrobe and get into the
animal's watering trough to soap off. Dad was put
out 'cause the stock would not drink and he had to
bucket the solution out and pump new water in.
Even so it was a few days before everything was
back to normal.

After Brownie Bob had quit rolling in the flower
garden and biting the petunias, this particular
summer had passed and school had started. I had
some hunting adventures without Brownie Bob.
There was a rash of newly made badger holes, so I
gets me a couple of coyote #3 traps and make the
sets and sure enough, the next night after school I
have me a badger. But brother what a problem, I

don't dare get even close to him. Necessity being the
mother of invention, I throws a lariat loop over the
badger to where it comes tight on the chain and then
by the horn on my saddle I pull him, stake, and trap
home. The combination has to be wrapped around an
apple tree so a body can get close enough to do him
in. An old bed post was handy so I whopped him over
the bean with it. He shuddered and lay still so with
my trusty Barlow knife I picked up a leg and jabbed
it with the point and *resurrection*! He came to with a
woof that put a biting sow to shame. Thank goodness
he was still in the trap. I was convinced there was
going to have to be other arrangements made before
he was going to part with his coat. The .22 rifle did
the trick. I butchered his hide off and again Mom
made me bathe and it wasn't even Saturday night.
The following night I scored again but it was a
skunk. I think that critter had already expended his
supply of perfume. This time I was prepared with
the little .22 Winchester and I plinked him, but I
also knew better than to closely communicate with
him. So by roping skunk and trap, I led him to the
neighbor's yard, and gave one of them kids a nickel
to take him out of my trap. I led the empty trap
home on the end of a 35 foot lariat.

While Brownie Bob was still just plain Brownie, I
built him a harness and taught him to pull me in the
red wagon, then the sleigh, come winter. The only
speed he knew was as fast as he could go. He did not
know "Gee!" or "Haw!" or "Mush!" but responded to
horse language. There was always a baking powder
biscuit or similar reward after a trip.

The neighbors had a huge Great Dane dog. I was playing with the two dogs when the big Dane reared up and put his paws on my back. Brownie Bob did not cater to such playing and from behind, and neutered the big Dane.

This Brownie Bob dog, to my knowledge has never been duplicated or equaled. Through Louie Cohan, a hide salvage buyer, we discovered an outlet for our pelts. Brownie Bob and I made this trapping an every-afternoon business. It got to the point where if I was kept in after school, Brownie would go inspect our traps anyhow. As a matter of fact, later on all I had to do was set out a stretcher board with scent by it and he would bring back the fur-bearing critter it smelled like and fit the stretcher board. Everything went fine until one warm fall afternoon mother Nelson put out a bucket with my little sister's nasty diaper in it and then set up the ironing board by it and we never saw Brownie Bob since.

About that same time there was a rash of communicable itch going around. You would see most everyone secretly scratching, and it would feel so good too. Mom would mix a sulfur and lard paste and apply it generously to be rubbed in. We affected ones would rub each other and really, was quite enjoyable. But if you stood too close to the school heater the lard would warm and the sulfur would smell and you would itch. But I had the perfect alibi; the smell was due to my trapping.

The Man My Dog Thinks I Am

I pray I'm the sort of cowboy
that folks like to be around;
A fellow that helps those in need
and picks them up off the ground.

I try to be the kind that would
help others out of a jam;
And I hope I can be just half
the man my dog thinks I am.

That's right, my dog thinks I'm the best
and that I can do no wrong;
He thinks I'm kind to everyone,
honest as the day is long.

To him I am the chuckwagon,
each morning and afternoon;
I am his friend and confidante,
And he thinks I hung the moon.

He believes I am all knowing,
I am perfect and all wise;
He thinks I'd never disparage,
or gossip like other guys.

He worships the ground I walk on,
looks on me with loyal eyes,
And believes that I'm a cowboy,
who never boasts, brags or lies.

In the end when I am graded,
on my life's final exam;
I hope I have been at least half
the man my dog thinks I am.

Cowboy Glossary

Dad (far left) doctoring a sick calf

That's when Lem showed up, and offered his help,
see, he's a lot like a blister;
He usually appears, when the work is done,
then blows on out like a twister.

For dudes, tenderfeet, and those who just don't savvy our cowboy palaver, here's some help. *Alphabetical order? Cowboys don't have no stinking alphabetical order.*

Cowboy Glossary

- Sulled Up: Describes the attitude of an old cow that has decided not to respond to any stimulus in any form... kinda like an old married couple.

- Slick: An unbranded, unmarked calf ready for you to claim it. After you put your brand on it, hopefully it doesn't mother up to and suck the neighbor's cow.

- Dogie: An old term used in the past to describe an orphaned calf; used now almost exclusively by dudes, wannabes, and the occasional cowboy poet.

- McCarty: The gringo-ized version of the Spanish word "mecate," see *mecate*.

- Mecate: Horse hair braided rope incorporated into a bridle system and ties to the bosal, see *Bosal*.

- Bosal: The nose piece (usually made from rawhide) that is attached to the headstall, see *Headstall (this could go on all day)*.

U Headstall: The part of the bridle that sets on the top of the horse's head and holds either the bosal or bit *(that's it, no more!)*.

U Ringy: Used normally when referring to wild, unpredictable cattle but can also describe certain cowboys quite sufficiently.

U Cull: Cattle cut out of the herd to be shipped, sold, or eaten. Not necessarily in that order.

U Day Worker: Used loosely to describe a cowboy who works on a day-to-day basis for various outfits in various capacities. Fear of commitment may be an issue for this cowboy.

U Whoa Nellie: To put the "Whoa Nellie" on something is to stop it immediately, if not sooner.

U Heavies: Not referring to the cowboys after a branding dinner, but it refers to gravid cows (cows in the motherly way).

U Open: Cows that are not in the motherly way and are usually in danger of being "culled" *(see above)*.

U Heifers: Young cows that have never given birth before, unless of course you are talking about second year heifers, which is kind of a misnomer. It's sort of like being a second year virgin.

◡ <u>Dally:</u> Another gringo-ization combining the Spanish words "Dar la vuelta" which roughly means to "take a turn around." That's what cowboys do with the free end of their ropes after catching an animal: they dally around the saddle horn, all the while trying not to lose a thumb.

◡ <u>Gelding:</u> A stud horse who has lost his procreative privileges *(enough said)*.

◡ <u>Green Broke:</u> A young horse that has been saddled up and ridden "X" amount of times. The "X" could be three or thirty... depends if you are the buyer or the seller.

◡ <u>Remuda:</u> Along with the word "Cavvy," a fancy word for a herd of ranch horses. Using this word might also give the person who owns only one horse a sense of belonging.

◡ <u>Cinchy:</u> Describes a horse that gets a little snotty when the saddle is tightened down or a cowboy that is faced with a marriage proposal.

◡ <u>Grab Leather:</u> Also known as "choking the horn" or "sucking the pacifier." If a fresh mount busts in two with you on it, there's no shame in grabbing leather to stay in the saddle. Just expect some good natured ribbing if you are caught.

◡ <u>Jingle the Horses:</u> The cowboy who gets to bring the horses in for the day's work, jingles the horses. He is blessed with the sights, sounds, and smells that few other people ever experience... mainly because it is done at 4 o'clock in the morning!

ʊ Leggins: The Texas way of saying chaps, which is the Wyoming way of saying chinks, which is the Nevada way of saying leggins.

ʊ Mugger/Wrestler: The feller at brandings who throws and holds the calves while the more skilled folks do the other work. These cowboys usually wear a size 2 hat and size 40 shirt.

ʊ Norther: A cold north wind usually accompanied by a nasty storm. It is a quick way of describing to others the perils of pending disaster and also sounds really cool when used in Western movies and songs.

ʊ Packing the Mail: To ride at full speed, much like the Pony Express of old while resembling the Postal Service of today since employees of both organizations pack weapons.

ʊ Off His Feed: Refers to an animal that is sick or a cowboy with a hangover.

ʊ Rig: The short term a cowboy uses to describe his saddle and sometimes his pickup, both of which are molded to the cowboy's hind end and can often rub him the wrong way.

- ☾ Piggin' String: A short piece of rope used to tie three of the four feet on a calf/steer/cow while a cowboy/cowgirl/ranch hand, doctors/marks/otherwise harasses the animal.

- ☾ Calf Fries: The first cut off a prime beef. The by-product of making a bull calf into a steer. A cowboy delicacy also referred to as "Rocky Mountain oysters."

- ☾ Houlihan: An overhand loop thrown most effectively in close quarters where the cowboy does not want to stir up the herd. *Results may vary, void where prohibited.*

- ☾ Riding Drag: Does not reference cowboys who prefer riding in dresses, but is the cowboy charged with pushing the cattle from the back of the herd.

- ☾ Tie Hard and Fast: The anti-dally. Tying the free end of a rope to the saddle horn in a manner that it will not, in any circumstance, come loose. It's a lot like being on the business end of a live, thousand pound yo-yo.

Service with a Smile

The morning was crisp, the weather was calm,
it was time for equine breeding;
The stud was ready, the mares were in heat,
and we had finished the feeding.

That's when Lem showed up, and offered his help,
see, he's a lot like a blister;
He usually appears, when the work is done,
then blows on out like a twister.

He just wants to come for donuts and pop
and closely times his arrival;
Today he was wrong, the day finally came
for some work-ethic revival.

Lem don't know much 'bout equine husbandry,
but today I could use a hand;
I need both of mine and all of my wits
in making this randy horse stand.

I accepted his help, with some reservation,
but my deepest fears were valid,
Cuz poor ol' Lem is one banana shy
of making a whole fruit salad.

I said, "I need aid, in covering the mares,"
If he'd help, I'd be in his debt;
He stood there confused, with nary a word,
and broke out with an ice-cold sweat.

He asked, "What's the pay," I tell him, "For this,
Ma's chicken fried steak and some beans";
He jumped at the bait, like a frog at a fly,
then asked me what "covering" means.

Impatient, I sneered and answered abrupt,
not using the best choice of words;
"I'm going to breed my daughter's paint mare,
Then work my way back through the herds."

His eyes glazed over, with a thousand-yard stare,
I could tell something was amiss;
He swallowed real hard, and asked me straight out,
"Does your wife know you're doing this?"

16

Christmas Remembered

Dad with one of his fine-looking buckskin mares
on the Land Ranch

*There will be no sleigh, on this Christmas day,
instead he will come in a coach;
Pulled again this year, but not by reindeer,
some horses will bring his approach.*

Written by James F. Walker Nelson

I think it appropriate to acquaint some "New Timers" with that pair of "Old Timers" Jack and Emily Tooth. Jack was one you wanted to have on your side if a Saturday night brawl erupted. And Emily (Madame Queen) was as sharp and cutting with her tongue as was her humor, not to be put in print. If crossed or double crossed, either could be like a biting sow protecting the kids.

They had a disastrous house fire at Golden Valley that took their three children, plus a neighbor girl who had come to spend the night while Jack and Emily came to town.

At old time dances, Jack and Emily were star performers. They danced enthusiastically for years. They were long-time friends of my father and mother.

The time of the year triggers this writing. The winter of 1948 and 1949 has long been remembered by many. Jack and I had summered six or eight horses on the Bill Tracy property adjacent to the old California/Oregon trail junction up Birch Creek twenty some miles from town. J.C. Price and families had a dry farm immediately west of Tracy. School was still maintained at the Junction or Moulton.

It was pushing Christmas time when Jack and I loaded a couple of saddle horses in a truck headed up Birch Creek. We made it about half way when we were forced to park the truck and take to the deepening snow on horseback. We soon had to quit the road to take to the brush where it had not drifted. We tracked one another, making a broken path to come out on. We only made it there by nearly dark.

The Prices opened their dugout house to us, which we gratefully accepted. There was a feed of rye for our saddle horses and an old abandoned building on the Tracy property provided shelter for the horses. We proceeded to the dugout for a surprisingly good meal and a comfortable night.

After steak and rye cakes for breakfast, the kids took off for school on a well-beaten path. I think there were eleven of them. Two families had joined, making one. You could hear them all the way to the school a mile away.

Mail delivery had ceased. A horse with sleigh on an unbroken road was out of the question. Jack and I made it back to Oakley with the horses before dark that day. The horses were eager to leave the snow country and followed our blazed trail with no problem.

Jack and I, a day or two later, took a suggestion with us to the Burley Elks Club. I'm not sure what the Elks fixed up but they chartered Ken Roundy and his Cessna 180 airplane to deliver some packages of Christmas gifts to the Price family. The day before Christmas was a beautiful sunny, calm day. Jack accompanied the chartered airplane "Santa" to the Price's dooryard and kicked the carton of goodies nearly down the Price's chimney. A Christmas remembered.

Side Note:

Along with an absolute heart of gold, Dad also had a wonderful, twisted sense of humor and he often enlisted Mom's help in sharing it with others. If I may inject here, Mom enjoyed the occasional prank every bit as much as Dad. This can be demonstrated by the Christmas card Dad asked Mom to reproduce on a piece of scrap wallpaper and send to our friends and neighbors. The card was received in the spirit which it was intended by most, but there were a few that just didn't get the joke. Mom ran into a neighbor fellow a few days later, who offered her a twenty dollar bill to help us out through Christmas. What a sweet, naïve old feller.

MONEY is SCARCE
TIMES ARE hard
HERE's youR damned old
ChRistMAS CaRd.

MERRy ChristMAS.

I'm wRiting this note to REMind you
ThAt in flation hAs tAKEN AWAy

The things that I hold most EssEntiAl
my woRKShop, my REindEER And sleigh.

Now I'm making my Rounds on a donKEy
H's old, hE's CRipplEd And slow,

So you'll Know if I don't SEE you At ChRistMAS
ThAt I'm out on my Ass in the snow.

MERRy ChristMAS
HAppy New YEAR
SantA Claus

Santa's Hired Hand

Santa's been busy, runs himself dizzy,
each Christmas he falls way behind;
So, to help him out, with his western route,
he hired a cowboy of some kind.

A few things will change, out there on the range,
but presents will come all the same;
So please be advised, and don't be surprised,
this year is a whole different game.

There will be no sleigh, on this Christmas day,
instead he will come in a coach;
Pulled again this year, but not by reindeer,
some horses will bring his approach.

You'll not hear a shout, echoing about,
Dasher, Dancer, Prancer and such;
As Bonnie and Clyde, take over the ride,
along with Jim, Jake, Dom, and Dutch.

The only glowing nose, is the one that goes,
on the face of Santa's new hand;
'Cause it's cold out there, in sub-zero air,
as he rides for the North Pole brand.

It gets awful cold, the reins hard to hold,
so please have hot coffee with cream;
Leave beef steak instead, of cookies and bread,
and oats for the rest of his team.

He don't really care, for "carols" out there,
he likes cowboy poetry best;
So play a few tracks, from Mitchell or Bax,
Kiskaddon, Clark, Barker or Guest.

He goes straight to work, with nary a shirk,
and fills the stockings 'til they heave;
With a few hoof picks, mineral salt licks,
worm paste, and a new AI sleeve.

His Wranglers fit loose, about his caboose,
when putting the presents away;
As he drops his sack, he'll expose his crack,
In a crude and awkward display.

Icicles are formed, as the air is warmed,
on his 'stache that used to be black;
A dog is his elf, and rides by himself,
with the toys stuffed in a grain sack.

The Grinch doesn't dare come in anywhere,
Santa's hired hand might be roaming;
He packs a long Colt, and a Sharps quick bolt,
and learned to shoot in Wyoming.

He's the best hired hand in all of the land,
though you'll not see a stranger sight;
When he shouts his call, "Merry Christmas y'all,
and to alla y'all a good night!"

17

The Endangered Cowboy

Dad with my sister Doris

Old West Riders, Up-All-Nighters,
and them handy with a rope;
Nighthawk Watchers, Gun Handle Notchers,
and those who fear bars of soap.

Dad was an insomniac. He would be awake in the
wee hours of the morning listening to the farm
market report and brewing coffee on the wood-
burning kitchen stove before the roosters even
thought about waking up to crow. I must have
inherited that cursed malady from him.

Some nights I have a whale of a time getting to
sleep, as was the case the night I researched the
Endangered Species Act (ESA). Yep, that's right,
with nothing better to do, I surfed the worldwide
web in search of a literary sedative. I had never read
the ESA and never really had an uncontrollable urge
to do so, but this night I must have been in a pensive
and philosophical mood... or had a terrible case of
indigestion, one or the other. I was never a big fan of
the ESA, as I felt it encroached a bit too much on
honest folks who struggled to make a living in the
agriculture industry. Ergo, I felt compelled to read
the ESA and either validate my philosophy by
becoming an informed critic or change my
philosophy by joining the cause.

Neither happened for me, because as I read the act
to the end I was left asking the question, what about
the endangered cowboy? I believe he and his
heritage to be worthy of protection. Therefore, I took
a couple of sections of the ESA and where it said
plant, animal, or *species,* and I inserted the word
cowboy.

The following are excerpts from the new and improved
Endangered <u>Cowboy</u> Act:

US Code Title 16, Chapter 35, Section 1531.
Congressional Findings and Declaration of Purposes and Policy.

The Congress finds and declares that:

(1) Various species of Cowboy in the United States have been rendered extinct as a consequence of economic growth and development untempered by adequate concern and conservation;

(2) Other species of Cowboy have been so depleted in numbers that they are in danger of or threatened with extinction;

(3) These species of Cowboy are of esthetic, ecological, educational, historical, recreational, and scientific value to the Nation and its people;

(4) The United States has pledged itself as a sovereign state in the international community to conserve to the extent practicable the various species of Cowboy facing extinction.

US Code Title 16, Chapter 35, Sec. 1533.
The Determination of Endangered Cowboys and Threatened Cowboys.

The Secretary shall by regulation promulgated in accordance with subsection (b) of this section determine whether any Cowboy is an endangered Cowboy or a threatened Cowboy because of any of the following factors:

(a) The present or threatened destruction, modification, or curtailment of his habitat or range

(b) Overutilization for commercial, recreational, scientific, or educational purposes

(c) Disease or predation

(d) The inadequacy of existing regulatory mechanisms; or

(e) Other natural or manmade factors affecting his continued existence

With the substitution of the word *cowboy*, this act finally made good sense to me. Later on in the ESA, the article went on to provide their definition of various endangered species. Of course, I would have to provide a definition of my own.

Defining the Endangered Cowboy

Quarter-Horse Nuts, Tight Wrangler Butts,
and Calvers on cold spring nights;
Old Pickup Trucks, a horse that bucks,
and Scrappers not afraid of fights.

Old West Riders, Up-All-Nighters,
and them handy with a rope;
Nighthawk Watchers, Gun Handle Notchers,
and those who fear bars of soap.

Island Paniolos, Dry-land Vaqueros,
and Beef Producers of the Rockies;
Fishin' Line Danglers, Tyson Chicken Wranglers,
and Farmers with Walkie-Talkies.

Cowboy Poets, Horseshoe Throw-Its,
And Association Saddle Riders;
Seasoned Farriers, Horse Tack Carriers,
and even some afraid of spiders.

Northern Agrarians, Stockyard Librarians,
And Shepherds of the old Southwest;
Tall Turkey Talkers, Tennessee Walkers,
and recipients of much needed rest.

Sandhill Grazers, Catahoula Raisers,
and even Hog Wrestlers to boot;
Coyote Catchers, Border Collie Fetchers,
and Geezers that don't give a hoot.

Everglade Waders, Dances with Gators,
and a Cajun to fill yer quotas;
Grain Combiners, Tough Coal Miners,
and Ranchers from both the Dakotas.

Alberta Chinookers, Calf Fry Cookers,
and the B.C. Throwers of Twine;
Calgary Stampeders, 4-H Leaders
all north of the Medicine Line.

Real Mule Skinners, no Lottery Winners,
a Brand Inspector to keep it all straight;
Expert Horse Trainers, Little Neck Reiners,
and St. Pete at the Golden Gate.

Feed Store Runners, Battleship Gunners,
and all of our Troops at war;
Full Time Vets, Part Time Pets,
and taxes to keep us all poor.

Them Old Texicans, them New Mexicans,
and Hoppy, Gene, and Roy;
Good people all, Great and/or Small,
defines the endangered Cowboy.

A Few Short Stories
And Observations

Dad atop the hay stack

The room is freezing, the throne keeps teasing,
and you don't want to leave your bed;
As more time passes, your fear amasses,
of that ice-cold sprint to the head.

Written by James F. Walker Nelson

During the Dust Bowl days (How come the
Footballers don't play in one of those?) there were
many "Grapes of Wrath" caravans come through this
part of the California and Oregon Trail country.
Some of them could have put Jack and the Beanstalk
tales to shame. May I relate one of the popcorn stalk.
Seems as though this Missourian was cultivating a
popcorn field and it was so dry and hot the corn ears
began to pop. They literally exploded. A regular
hailstorm of popped corn. The mules thought it was
snow and froze to death.

U

This sheepherder story has to do with a witty gent
and a relative to many of us Twin-Cassia residents,
and of the time of poor refrigeration. The sheepman's
wife had a lump of butter go rancid and rather than
throw it out, sent it with the camp-tender to the
herder. The next trip to camp the camp-jack asked
about the butter. "Oh, I would throw it out to the dog
while I ate and then throw it back in the camp while
the dog ate."

U

My uncle Don was working for the old Utah
Construction Co., probably on the Boar's Nest. He
disliked any kind of labor one could not get done
from the saddle. It came haying time and Jimmy
Zilcox put him on the lead mower to open up the
rough meadows. Don knew all the beaver holes and
other obstacles to be cut around. This was not to
Don's liking howsomever. The horses were a good
gentle and reliable pair, but they were around a
willowy bend in the creek. Don cut himself a good

green willow and proceeded to give the horses a good tuning up, and stepped off the mower, headed them for the corral, and threw the lines at them. Of course they went right to the corral and stopped. Don came limping in after them. Jimmy met him and wondered how they got started. "Wal Jimmy, from where I sat, it looked like they waz even."

℧

The production lines with their efficiency experts prohibit the development of practical down-to-earth humor such as covering fresh cow dung with dust and then calling the young kids around to see you put a dime in the center of it. Then step back about 30 yards to toe the line for a get ready, set, go!

℧

Everyone attended the old time dances, including babies. The babes were wrapped in blankets and put to bed on benches that were turned face-to-face. The big mix up there was after the folks got home and found that someone at the dance had scrambled the kids.

℧

One of the most impressive public speakers made a quote that has stayed with me for a long time. He cleared the throat and stated, "Before I begin this speech, I would like to say something." This should be put in every official's "must" box.

℧

This small but historic town of Oakley boasts some real personalized characters. There are some possessed with an insatiable desire to break into a conversation whether welcome or not. They possess a memory of an elephant but repeatedly cannot remember anything relating incidents, like one gent

in particular. There were three of us at the coffee
counter: Dave, myself, and a Garret truck delivery
man. Dave and I have partnered up on various small
contract jobs. We were discussing one when Henry
came in. We acknowledged him and that was just
the same as inviting him to sit down and let the
spring loose on his lower jaw. Henry is 72 or 73 years
and very active and insists on relating his early days
at home. For the 11-teenth time he started his
rehearsal of an old couple whose ages extended into
the 90's and were able still to dress and care for
themselves. "Remarkable, Henry, remarkable. But
did I ever tell you of my grandfather Nelson?" "No I
don't remember you mentioning him." "Well Hen he
was shot to death at the age of 102 by a jealous
husband." The trucker blew coffee over the counter,
Dave snorted, and good 'ol Henry retreated.

B. Shindler cci

Ode to the Running Commode

The bunkhouse can be, an absolute sea,
of smells and the strangest of sights;
But that ain't the worst, the whole place is cursed,
with sounds when you turn out the lights.

It will encumber, your rest and slumber,
and it makes you reach for your robe;
It's the bane of man, and a plague that can,
test even the patience of Job.

Your work clothes are doffed, you finally drift off,
you're lying there perfectly still;
When after its use, all Hades breaks loose,
The toilet starts running at will.

It wails a sad tune, this lonesome bassoon,
blown by the wee tidy bowl man;
The noise is grating, you end up hating,
the person who last used the can.

You are warm and sound, your bedroll unwound,
right after mid-wifing a cow;
The bowl's to the brim, left running by him,
it's a case of principle now.

The room is freezing, the throne keeps teasing,
and you don't want to leave your bed;
As more time passes, your fear amasses,
of that ice-cold sprint to the head.

You're not getting up, it's that selfish pup,
who should silence the beast within;
You'll lay there and stew, the commode and you,
'til someone finally gives in.

So now you can't sleep, you tried counting sheep,
but the privy proceeds to run;
That porcelain croon has got to end soon,
your patience is just about done.

It pricks at your ears, and brings you to tears,
you've had better nights' sleep in camp;
The ceramic bowl, continues to toll,
causing your tympanum to cramp.

Your temples are sore, can't take it no more,
and your head is going berserk;
Your thoughts are spastic, the scene is drastic,
you're ready to shoot that darn jerk.

You see him right there, asleep without care,
through the soft light of a candle;
You cuss at the stream, and finally you scream,
"Somebody jiggle the handle!"

In spite of your sighs, nobody replies,
you alone must stifle the flow;
You sprint to the pot, then back in your cot,
just to find... now you have to go!

19

Shoeing Rigs

One of Dad's International Harvester shoeing rigs

But it gets me on time to each shoeing gig
and though it's lost its original shine;
The truth be known...I sure like that rig
and it's been paid for since '79.

I don't know how he did it, but Dad could make the vehicles he drove go anywhere he wanted to go. Simply put, he drove them like he rode a horse: uphill against a 20% two track grade, in and out of a cloudburst-carved arroyo, traversing across a shale slide, or following a livestock trail through giant sage brush (in southern Idaho, sagebrush can grow to be taller than a horse and his rider). As I think about it, trucks back then were not engineering marvels. They were simple, tough, and heavy. No extra thought went into suspension; suspension was for sissies. No extra thought went into mileage; mileage was for sissies. No extra thought went into comfort; comfort... well, you get the picture. A truck was made to last, nothing more and certainly nothing less. Just pop the hood on one of Dad's old trucks and you could see the ground underneath the engine, no added emissions control, air conditioning, or anti-theft devices, just a straight six with an oil bath air cleaner. Manly!

Dad's original choice of pickups were made by International Harvester. I think he owned two or three of these at different times. Then he went into his Chevrolet phase as the old IH pickups faded out. I swear, the people who designed these old trucks must have known farriers were going to drive them. Dad used his as a shoeing rig, mobile forge, tractor, snowmobile, stock truck, freight wagon, and family SUV, with no hesitations or reservations. I remember one particular family outing when the old IH pickup was transformed into an amphibious assault vehicle. It was better than James Bond. I mean real 007 stuff. I was too young to remember the particulars of it, but Dad drove the old beast through a beaver pond, with the family in transit. Yep, a beaver pond. I don't know why, other than to get to the other side... and because he could! I do remember seeing the water pour through the door cracks and spill onto the floorboard, but it drained out just as easily when we drove onto the opposite bank. Keep in mind, these old rigs were rear wheel drive. There was no such thing as four-wheel drive, and they must have weighed as much as a Sherman tank.

It was always extra exciting when the Sherman tank turned into a mobile home. Either for an over-nighter or just for a quick fishing trip up Fall Creek, the shoeing rig was ever faithful. The shoeing supplies were off-loaded at home and the army-surplus-box-turned-picnic-basket, fishing poles and bedrolls were loaded in the pickup bed... and so were we. It was more excitement than a young feller could stand, as the old truck rattled up the dugway toward the earth-filled dam that stifled Goose and Trapper Creeks and their tributaries, past the muddy reservoir, past the Badger Gulch switchback, past limestone cutaways, en route to where the shoeing rig became a roller coaster. That's right, the Trapper Creek Swells. Awesome! We had never seen a roller coaster until later in life, so we had no idea that was what we were experiencing. The anticipation was almost as electrifying as the swells. The Trapper Creek road crossed perpendicular to finger-like projections that angled down from the larger mountains, five or six in a row, creating an up-and-down stretch of road that would tickle the gizzard of even the most hardened crop duster. We would stand up in the back with our hands in the air as Dad accelerated through the bottom of the first gully to apex of the next finger, screaming "Faster, faster!" Each time we peaked, we'd chicken out and drop our hands, certain we were going to take flight. Then as quickly as we plummeted down the back side of each pinnacle, our ride was over. Our disappointment only lasted momentarily as we were reminded we still had to drive back through them in order to get home.

But, for the most part, Dad's truck hauled horse shoeing equipment, complete with anvil, stand, tools, shoes, nails, and a portable forge made out of the shell of an abandoned water heater. The water heater was cut in half in a horizontal manner, a door cut in the front, a blower hole cut in the side where a hose ran in connected to a hand-crank blower on the other end, and a vent cut in the top. It was truly a fine piece of workmanship in itself and was multifunctional. Not only did it serve as a hot forge for shaping horse shoes, it was frequently the branding iron fire and Radar Range for cooking the first cut off a prime beef—you know, mountain oysters. Being the dutiful young boys we were, big brother Jim and I were always the blower motors. The motors accelerated upon request and decelerated usually because of fatigue, but a constant air flow was requisite. Too fast and the metal shoes melted (emitting a beautiful *sparkler* effect I might add), too slow and all you had was a shoe too hot to hold with a bare hand. Turning the blower handle was an art, much akin to tuning a musical instrument. You couldn't tell how fast you were turning by simply watching the speed of the handle. You had to listen. A specific monotonous hum was the target speed, not a buzz or a whine, a hum.

Combined with the whirr of the impellor and the whistle of the air escaping through the hot coke, Dad's opus magnum culminated in the perfect horse shoe. It was magnificent.

Dad with one of his shoeing rigs

My Shoeing Rig

My horse shoeing truck is part primer gray,
and it is a *wonder* to behold;
I often *wonder*, will it start today,
and what's smoking on the manifold.

But it gets me on time to each shoeing gig
and though it's lost its original shine;
The truth be known...I sure like that rig
and it's been paid for since '79.

The old battery, well, it ain't "batt-ing"
and the air-intake needs a breather;
The generator, well, it ain't "gen-ing"
and the pistons, ain't... *working either*!

The radio squawks out one am station,
the seat has no springs underneath;
But the ride is real smooth...just a little vibration
that's been known to jar fillings from teeth.

The A/C works fine, when going to town,
and it runs on *240* power;
240 that is, with *two* windows down,
at over *forty* miles an hour.

There's a sack on the shift and mud on the floor,
a cup holder screwed to the dash;
Rocks in the ashtray, dog slobber on the door
and a check that I still need to cash.

The tailgate is gone, the cab light burned out
the paint is all gone from the bed;
There's dust in the vents and trash strewn about
and a fragrance like something is dead.

As a real looker, she ain't worth her sand,
in fact she is mighty low tech;
My GE nippers, my anvil and stand,
book higher than this poor old wreck.

The new nails I store, in an old ammo can,
and my tools in a green army box;
A spare tire in the back, from a Dodge minivan,
with some horseshoes and dirty old socks.

She's held together, with duct tape and wire,
and runs mainly on diesel and luck;
With the money I make, as a shoer for hire,
I sure can't afford a new truck.

So onward we go, just staying the course,
though some days I doubt she will make 'er;
And I've always said, if she were a horse,
not even the canner would take 'er.

20

Oakley in the '20s

Dad (infant) with his siblings, circa 1920

But he was patient in biding his time,
and calculated his revenge;
When one month later he plotted his crime,
as it came his chance to avenge.

Written by James F. Walker Nelson

The late Charles Young of Kimberly, formerly of
Oakley, was one good blacksmith. Most any kid of the
'20s and early '30s spent some time at his blacksmith
shop in Oakley (Idaho). His coal-fired forge and the
showering of hot metal sparks would hold me
spellbound by the hour when I was in town for any
reason. My father, Gus Nelson, would Model "T" to
the pool hall for a couple cans of Tuxedo and watch
the card games. That was in the good old days when
women and kids were not made welcome in man's
domain. The big blacksmith was just the opposite. In
his motherly manly way he made you feel quite at
home, even though he may have had some kind of
mischief in mind. He would tell you what he was
doing or what he was going to do to a piece of metal
and then go ahead and do it. I was particularly awed
by his horse shoeing. Those were precious visits to
me. Dad asked me once what I was going to be when I
grew up. "A blacksmith," I replied, without hesitation.

Oakley hosted a barber of cowboy vintage and
between the two shops one could get a college degree
in personality, each trying to outwit the other
"nitwit" (their expression). The druggist at the time
had a house—and store-spoiled dog. The barber and
cowboy farmer doctored up a box of chocolates with
croton oil. They were feeding them to the dog when
the smithy came by demanding a share, which he
was promptly made welcome to. This was even
better than they anticipated. Flush-water toilets
were a rare luxury and the smithy retired to the
raspberry patch, emerging with a berry rash second-

to-none. Imagine trying to dry-blot with green
raspberry bushes.

I was a lad most grownups tolerated and mother
Nelson once remarked she never did have a little boy
Jim. I liked being with my horse and dog or with the
grown men. The boys my age were not old enough
and the bigger boys irritated me. Someone asked
Gus Nelson how in the world he could turn a kid
loose as he did. He answered, "Hah! Kid and be
damned, we got no kid in our house."

I vividly recall pee'n the bed my last time (I think).
Dad and I had gone for a wagon load of wood and we
led an extra horse for dragging (no, not racing).
There were many wood haulers at the time and the
easy wood had been cleaned up. We took a hand plow
with us to plow a furrow in the uphill side for the
wagon wheels. We pulled the wagon as far as
possible and then Dad, with the team for jerking the
juniper trees, and me, with the drag horse, went on
to the top of the ridge. Dad jerked them over and I
dragged them down to the wagon riding Ol' Starr.

Well, one drag got to rolling on us and twisted the
chain and Starr's tugs, then Ol' Starr and me. I
bailed off, but the drag and Starr rolled on to the
bottom beyond the wagon. I sure got scared for Ol'
Starr, but after he got over being dizzy he got up still
somewhat groggy and fluffed up a bit. I was shaken
up more than the horse. I let him back up where Dad
was still a-jerkin'. He allowed that was some show
and next time I'd probably be smart enough to head
my horse uphill if it rolled again. Quite a bit of

telling goes with when you quit pee'n the bed. That night in bed, I was kind of foozy. I nightmared or nighthorsed all night and then dreamed I was pee'n against a log. But the log was Dad's leg.

And that's the way it was in Oakley during the '20s.

Stubby Higgins' Revenge

The unwritten law out here in the West,
to which cowboys try to adhere;
You don't tease the cook, not even in jest,
'tis the rule of any frontier.

Stubby Higgins was our cook at that point,
and not the best one around;
But at least he worked hard to clean the joint,
and never used food off the ground.

So when the cowhands sewed up his trap door,
in a fit of youthful prank;
I figured there wouldn't be peace any more,
and breakfast was sure to be rank.

But he was patient in biding his time,
and calculated his revenge;
When one month later he plotted his crime,
as it came his chance to avenge.

The boss man brought in a small crippled calf,
for Stubby to roast really nice;
He cooked it up with a sinister laugh,
yep, Stubby's revenge over rice.

The veal was quite tender and most tasty,
but the gravy hid the surprise;
Stubby Higgins' revenge would be hasty,
and double their effort in size.

He mixed in the drippings with pleasure,
some cod oil, prune juice and worm paste;
A handful of flaxseed for good measure,
then juniper berries for taste.

There was enough lube stewed in that gravy,
to make cold molasses come loose;
A big enough dose for the U.S. Navy,
or to wax the inside of a moose.

Careful not to serve any to the boss,
large portions he gave to the boys;
An hour after devouring the sauce,
they heard the most gosh awful noise.

Gasping and squealing, and reeling with pain,
all hands raced for the two-holer;
Stumbling and tumbling and somewhat insane,
like pins knocked down by a bowler.

But before he fixed this marvelous meal,
Stubby snuck out back like a mouse;
In prelude to serving his vengeful veal,
nailed the door shut on the outhouse.

All the boys complained the prank was too mean,
that Stubby's revenge was shady;
And no one came out of this smelling clean,
especially the laundry lady.

21

Nature's Gel Nightmare

Dad with big brother Jim

Both may appear harsh at first sight,
but subtle when put into use;
The hard edges have worn down some,
polished by the years of abuse.

Next to dad, my big brother Jim is the best farrier
I've ever seen. It's almost like he was foreordained to
shoe. He is more comfortable in the shoeing posture
than he is standing straight up. But since Jim and I
both quit shoeing full time, we have developed
impressive abdominal goiters. You know, our six-
packs have turned into kegs, but that doesn't keep us
from getting under our own horses. In fact, when we
squat to put a hoof between our legs now, the added
weight in the front pulls our lumbar spine into a
perfect lordosis (swayback) and our bellies can rest on
the front of our thighs, creating a more ergonomic
work posture and taxing our glutes and hamstrings
less. Perhaps there are some benefits to being out of
shape.

But I digress. Big brother Jim is the quintessential
farrier, quiet and calm around horses, yet diplomatic
and forthright around their owners. It is no wonder
his phone rang off the hook come every spring and it
is no surprise great horse shoeing stories are
abundant. Like the time a barn cat jumped off a pole
rail fence onto the back of a clabber-butted
quarterhorse Jim was under, creating a Tasmanian
Devil-like whirlwind, all the while with the owner
expelling her laughter and glee. Or the time when he
forgot to take off his wedding ring and the horse he
was shoeing decided to put his foot down and an
unbent/unclenched nail lodged between his finger and
the ring. Fortunately, the horse was seasoned and
just stood there peacefully with Jim's hand contorted
underneath him. Or the time Jim remembered the
wedding ring incident, took his ring off, placed it in
his shoeing truck, then forgot to put it back on after

work and swept it out onto the ground in an undisclosed location while cleaning his out his rig. Or the time after he put a new set of shoes on a horse, the horse walked over to a barbed wire fence, hooked a shoe in it, and popped it off with the owner witnessing the routine. Or the time Jim put a fresh set of shoes on a horse and the horse promptly walked away from the scene and died! Then of course there are the multiple strikes, bites, kicks and licks too numerous to recount. But my favorite story involves a caustic topical ointment.

Anyone who has spent any amount of time underneath a horse knows it is hard work. Your back hurts, your legs and butt burn, your hands get stiff, and your knees ache, especially after multiple shoeings in one setting. The day in reference was a hot, dry summer day in which Jim was shoeing at home. Not the usual place for Jim to shoe, but the owners were desperate and agreed to bring the horses to him. After a long morning of equine podiatrics, Jim retired to the house for something cold to drink and a light lunch. The light lunch because there were more horses yet to shoe and it is terribly hard to bend over a full belly. While sitting at the dinner table, Jim mentioned to mama that his back was awful stiff. Being the beautiful, dutiful wife she is, Tina mentioned some analgesic balm she brought home after her last trip to town to the chiropractor's office. After agreeing to a treatment regiment, Tina swabbed a generous amount on the small of Jim's back. It felt cool when first applied and then quickly warmed to a soothing sensation and his muscles started to relax. Treatment phase one was complete and successful, but treatment phase two was about to come to fruition. With lunch in him and his back feeling better, it was time to attack the rest of the day. Jim began shoeing again but now it was in the heat of the day. One inevitable fact of shoeing is that when you shoe, you sweat, which is usually not an issue, but the topical ointment in the small of Jim's back was about to become an issue in a hurry. Unaware of what was about to go down, *literally*, Jim was about to be lit up. The combination of being bent over, sweating profusely, and the excess atomic balm mixed quite a concoction there in the small of his back and when he stood up, everything went south! The boiling river cascaded south between Jim's vertical smile like a molten lava flow through the chasms of Maui's lava beds, setting fire to everything in its path. The fire alarms began screaming as the liquid hell-fire careened down through the valley of death and Jim was fearing the devil! Let me tell you a little something about this type of analgesic: water activates the ingredients and you can't wash it off. I swear, if he could, he would have drug his butt across the gravel like a pin-wormed puppy and I even saw him eyeballing New Fork Creek that runs there through the corrals. But knowing this would give only temporary relief and fuel the fire, he wiped off what he could with an old rag and toughed it out. I know it's not right to derive pleasure from other's misfortunes, but that was one of the funniest circumstances witnessed by man.

The Old Crockett Spurs

As long as I can remember,
the Crockett spurs belonged to Jim;
They're modest, yet very complex,
and remind me a lot of him.

Tempered through hard work and labor,
engraved with years of bad weather;
Forged from the iron of turmoil,
thick in the skin and the leather.

Perfectly balanced in function,
dependable when called on to work;
Precise when applied to the trade,
dangerous when used by a jerk.

Both may appear harsh at first sight,
but subtle when put into use;
The hard edges have worn down some,
polished by the years of abuse.

Not very flashy to look at,
and don't make a whole lot of noise;
Often overlooked by most folks,
except for real working cowboys.

As progress outlasts tradition,
an emotion within me stirs;
Heritage is a priceless gift,
like Jim... and those old Crockett spurs.

The Little Impish Gremlin

Dad, front at left, with the Gus Nelson family

And by the end of the branding,
the kids were all smattered with mud;
They blended into the catch pens,
all covered with manure and blood.

Written by James F. Walker Nelson

At some point while in grade school I noticed a kind of little impish gremlin kept cropping up in me and doing things and saying things that I would never do or say. We had some really good neighbors whom Dad liked and I liked, but Mother Nelson humphed at. Maybe so, because they built a little homemade beer (home brew) and bootlegged a little booze. This being the time of Prohibition, Mother (Cora) even frowned upon drugstore-bought root beer.

Calapucci with the cart and I made a pit stop at the neighbors' on a Sunday; their kids were out chasing chickens. Chicken every Sunday. One of the bigger kids caught an old, I mean old, Plymouth Rock rooster. Why it would have taken a week of stewing before you could stick a fork in the water of the Rock Rooster.

This gremlin opened his impish little mouth and nudged me in the ribs and motioned toward a camp in the orchard where a big, raw-boned sheepherder was snoring off some home brew. I took the squawking

Rock Rooster by the neck, legs, and wings and in the arms of Morpheus entered the dreams of the King. The old rooster had spurs three to four inches long. The gremlin put him under the snorer and turned everything loose but the tail. The old cock squawked and spurred something beeootiful. The air activated with arms, feet, and rooster. As I circled 'round under the apple trees occasionally glancing over my shoulder, I could see huge hands and size 14 shoes dangerously close to my neck and posterior. Not having to duck much to get under the tree limbs, I out-winded Frank King and kept a respectable distance thereafter, and I lived to crow about the occasion.

Our school lunches at the time ranged from a bread and bacon sandwich one day to bread and jelly the next, then for variety a baking powder biscuit with a pork steak, and so on. One big kid who lived close, his Pa was the game warden, would bring his lunch in a gallon bucket with milk and dessert and stuff. Can't say we were exactly envious because his dad was on the state payroll to keep our dads in line. But one morning I came across a lame mallard duck and conked him on the bean, which was a state and federal offense. I stuffed him under my bibs and walked the rest of the way in through the field and hid the mallard drake behind the outhouse, then after recess and before noon I held up the customary two-finger signal. The big game warden's kid always hid his gallon lunch bucket in the shade through a hole under the school building. The little gremlin kept telling me that it was actually the thing to do, so I followed his instructions by removing all those good things to eat from his lunch bucket and put the pretty drake duck in and closed the lid. Back inside I did my

level darnedest to concentrate on studies and not
fidget. The last five minutes took at least an hour.
Finally the principal rang the bell and we marched
out row-by-row, my how slow, but I was glad to be the
last one and got there just in time to see the
expression on the big kid's face. The next five minutes
was worth all the lunch hours spent a-watching him
munching store bought bologna, peanut butter
sandwiches, cookies, and milk. To top it all off, there
was an imaginary line which dissected the girls from
the boys and an infraction of that rule meant a
measuring with a three-eighths inch yardstick. Some
of the more intrepid girls crossed the out-of-bounds
line to see what all the commotion was about and
better still, there was even a stiffer penalty for
profanity. Needless to say, the big kid was known as
"Duck" as long as he was in Oakley and he couldn't
whip all of us. Sometimes he was greeted with a
"quack, quack" instead of plain "Ducky Wucky." I
think he smelled a mouse but the absolute truth has
never been let out. To my knowledge, the little
gremlin did it and was worth every down feather of it.

Duck's warden father had a small cow-calf operation
on the Goose Creek some 25 miles south of Oakley in
the vicinity of several small distilleries of the
forbidden spirits. This was still in the Prohibition
days of small-time Al Capones and the warden's
brother Zeke was Oakley's town marshal. The
stoolpigeon would tip his brother off on shipments of
illegal spirits until one of the most harassed
bootleggers informed the pair of law enforcement
officers that he personally knew how the milk cow
"Dolly" came to mother several calves each season.

The Bare Facts

"Honest Officer, that's no lie,"
said Billy in pleading his case;
The lawman wasn't buying it,
and stood with a frown-embossed face.

But when the policeman stopped him,
with two other half-naked youth
in his car, stripped to their skivvies,
he simply had to tell the truth.

Billy and two of his siblings,
were helping the neighbor ranch brand;
Wrestling and holding the calves,
and generally lending a hand.

That spring was really a wet one,
with puddles and mud bogs galore;
The pens were all sloppy and slick,
like a home with piggy decor.

And by the end of the branding,
the kids were all smattered with mud;
They blended into the catch pens,
covered with manure and blood.

Having driven them out to brand,
in what Bill calls the "Date-mobile";
He didn't want to soil his car,
and ruin its sexy appeal.

He ordered the kids to disrobe,
leaving only their underwear;
Then he put their clothes in the trunk,
and gave them a blanket to share.

Bill also shucked his dirty duds,
and darted to the driver's seat;
Started the engine, dropped the clutch,
and commenced to pour on the heat.

Off to the house they burned rubber,
traveling faster than he should;
And when he saw a police car,
he figured this couldn't be good.

'Cause all their clothes were in the trunk,
out of reach and sure out of sight;
The gendarme pulled Billy over,
with a red and blue flashing light.

Billy tried hard to explain why
they were caught in this tactless gaffe;
When through a serious facade,
the trooper broke into a laugh.

The cops were called by the neighbors,
as a joke to play on young Bill;
They figured they'd get a good laugh,
and the cops might get a cheap thrill.

But the practical joke backfired,
and the whole thing turned out shady;
When Bill failed to see the humor,
'cause the trooper was a lady.

23

Missed a Good Opportunity

Kids patiently waiting as Dad saddles a pony

So I put the sneak on him from behind
and tom-hawked him over the head;
He dropped like a wet sack of cow manure,
and I was certain he was dead.

Growing up, big brother Jim and I sure missed out
on a lot of good opportunities to kill ourselves. I'm
not trying to be morbid; I'm just stating that because
of some stupid things we did, there were some real
opportunities to cash it in. You know, the only thing
keeping us alive was a mother's daily prayer, "... and
please guard and protect the boys as they go about
doing stupid things." The good Lord instilled fear in
man to keep him alive. Unfortunately, fear is often
snuffed out by fear's mortal enemy, machismo.

Many such opportunities come to mind, but one of
my favorites was the rawhide race. Every year the
local rodeo club, the Oakley Vigilantes, sponsored a
Gymkhana, in which young horsemen could display
their wide range of skills in equestrian events. There
were many events—the sack race, the egg carry, the
flag race—but the one event that captivated every
young rider's fancy was the rawhide race. It was a
test of manhood, or womanhood, as it turned out this
particular year; one girl signed up for the race. The
equipment consisted of a dried cow hide—not tanned
and hair still on the one side—wired to a short
section of lodge pole pine, to which a lariat was then
attached. Two people per team were required, one
person horseback and the other as the hide rider.
The loose end of the lariat was then dallied around
the horn. The rules were simple: two teams ran at
the same time, the horse and rider pulled the hide
and rider from one end of the arena, around a barrel
and back to the starting point. All the hide skinner
had to do was stay on... simple.

Well, this was big brother Jim's and my first year in this particular competition, because Mom wouldn't sign the consent form in the past. But this year we didn't tell Mom and got Dad to sign it (which he did with gusto). Jim was elected to be the dragger, because he was the only one with a horse big enough to pull a human on a cowhide across the gravel pit we called an arena. Therefore, I had the dubious distinction of being the hide skinner. Big brother Jim's instructions to me were short and succinct, "Don't let go." As we lined up at the end of the arena, I eyed down our competition. The other hide skinner was a girl! This promised to be one heckuva first outing for the Nelson boys, I thought to myself, but then I watched as she "geared-up" for the race. Now wait a doggone minute, she was putting on her Dad's coveralls, his leather gloves adorned her hands, and she was donning a motorcycle helmet with an acrylic face guard. That was the first time in my life I remember experiencing firsthand an "Oh No" moment. You know, that moment in time when you realize something really bad is about to happen and you instinctively blurt out the words, "Oh No." Before I could object to the unfair circumstances, the starting horn sounded and we were off. Gravel and dirt mixed with bucking stock manure pelted me like a spring hail storm and all I could do was close my eyes and grit my teeth. I had no idea if we were winning or not. I could see nothing and all I could hear was the sound of the rocks and dirt passing over and under the cowhide. Then I came to my senses long enough to realize we should be turning around the barrel soon. At that precise millisecond I felt the inside of the hide begin to raise off the ground. A pertinent piece of information that was not shared with me before the race was this: as the horse started to make the turn, you had to slide your body to the inside of the hide and even hang a knee off or the hide and you would tumble. Well, the hide and I tumbled. Sometimes I was riding the hide, other times the hide was riding me, and being the diligent brother that I was, I heard big brother Jim's voice in my head, "Don't let go." So I didn't. I finally ended up on top of the hide again and we crossed the finish line. A pertinent piece of information that was not shared with Jim before the race was this: Don't dump your dally while still running at full speed or the hide skinner will continue to slide after the hide stops moving. Well, Jim dropped his dally while still running and I slid off the front of the hide and through the arena another 20 feet. The furrow I left couldn't have looked any better than if it were made by a v-plow. To rub salt in the wound, as I looked up through dust-caked eyes, the girl was on her feet and out of her overalls accepting the starter's congratulations. She had done this before!

My pride was hurt, but not nearly as bad as my body was. I had an unbelievable road-rash on my arms and in the small of my back where my shirt had pulled up and my pants pulled down during one of my death-rolls with the cow hide. My shirt took about three years worth of wear in 30 seconds, I had 20 pounds of gravel stuffed down my britches, and because I gritted my teeth the whole way, my mouth was full of arena and it tasted like I had gargled with kitty litter.

The rawhide race was not the only opportunity the
good Lord had to take me home. There was the time
the cinch broke on my old McClellan saddle as I was
riding hell-bent-for-leather on a runaway horse; or
the time I was riding bareback and barefoot and
went through a barbed wire fence; or the time we put
a flank strap on one of our ponies and bucked him
out of the rodeo arena chutes; or the time when...
etc. etc. etc.

Playing Cowboys and Indians

Money sure was tight when we were just kids,
'twas tough but we didn't know it;
Our Mother and Dad did the best they could,
to provide and not to show it.

We had most of the things a child could want,
and always had clean clothes to wear;
We were mostly neat and were always pressed,
and Mom made sure we combed our hair.

My brother was nine and I was seven,
our birthdays came in September;
We celebrated the same month each year,
and were something to remember.

It seemed that year was especially tight,
so Dad carved us two wooden guns;
Hardwood two-by-fours made into rifles,
they were stout and durable ones.

Then we would play cowboys and Indians,
for hours and days upon end;
It wasn't long 'til those old wooden guns,
were mine and my brother's best friend.

Then the day came when I had him pinned down,
there was no escaping my fire;
Each time he would move I would shoot him dead,
and that added fuel to his ire.

I had him covered from every angle,
ol' pale face could not escape now;
There's no way he could get out of this one,
not this time, no way and no how!

But then he pulled an ace out of his sleeve,
and changed the rules amidst the fight;
He said I had run plum out of bullets,
and my lever was jammed up tight.

Well, if I had run clean out of bullets,
and my gun's action was stuck shut;
I'd have to do what the movie stars did,
hit him on the head with the butt!

So I put the sneak on him from behind
and tom-hawked him over the head;
He dropped like a wet sack of cow manure,
and I was certain he was dead.

I heard the loud "crack" echo off the barn,
but I hadn't broken my gun;
I'd knocked him out cold and he didn't move,
so I dropped my weapon and run.

There would be a posse tracking me soon,
they'd be bringing their hanging loops;
I had done it now, I was in way deep,
Mom would be calling out the troops.

I sought refuge in the tack shed out back,
and barricaded me inside;

My brother woke up and crawled to the house,
I prayed and continued to hide.

Mom closed up his cuts with butterfly strips,
and patched up his punkin' real nice;
Then gave him a glass of cold lemonade,
and packed his fat melon on ice.

She called out the scouts and sent out the crew,
for the maverick that scalped her son;
Told them to capture me dead or alive,
so I chose to stay on the run.

My sisters demanded my surrender,
but I wouldn't budge from my spot;
It wasn't 'til Mom sent out my brother,
I knew it was safe to be caught.

I spent some hard time locked in the pokey,
for this crime against my brother;
I was sentenced to a week's hard labor,
by the hanging judge, my mother.

But then the dust cleared, his head knots went down,
and the sight came back to his eyes;
My brother and I were right back at it,
fighting and shooting at bad guys.

But after the wreck new rules were installed,
and Mom laid down the law back then,
I was provided plenty of ammo,
and my gun never jammed again.

24

Gus and Cora Nelson

Dad's parents, Andrew Gustave and
Cora Brackett Nelson

*But this is right where my heart wants to be,
when it's my time to make that last ride;
Don't take me to town, just set my soul free,
it is here that I wish to abide.*

Written by James F. Walker Nelson

Andrew Gus Nelson was raised in the Grantsville,
Utah community. Through an association with the
Worthingtons, he went to Montana and helped bring
a bunch of horses to the Oakley valley, where his
older brother Swanty had already located. The turn of
the century is the only date I can give. Gus herded
these horses on to Trout and Swanty creeks. The
older brother Swanty was involved in the horses
somehow. Worthingtons had a contract with Uncle
Sam to furnish some horses to the cavalry with the
stipulation of "having been ridden." Gus rode 102
horses that winter and come spring the horses were
turned over to the cavalry as having been ridden.
Reports came back of it raining cavalry men all over
the fort.

This was in the era of open range and entrepreneurs
did nothing but grow and get big. Gus and Jim
Walker partnered up in sheep and later cattle. 'Twas
through this partnership that Gus and Cora met and
a mutual togetherness evolved. Jim Walker was later
unloaded from a beautiful black bronc his brother
Dave had given him, which resulted in his going over
the ridge to greener pastures, four days before my
birth. I can never remember of criticism of either
except there were some gentlemen who did not agree
when Gus and Mae Critchfield were selected by the
judges as the best dancers on the floor. Cora Nelson
was about the kindest person to ever grace these
green acres. I don't remember what I did wrong, but
she instructed me to bring a willow switch and come
to the house. I picked out a real good one but on the

way to the back porch, I thought I had made too good of choice in willows so I broke the switch in half. It still looked too wicked so I broke it again. By the time I reached the back porch, all that was left of a good willow switch was a twig.

I'll have to relate one incident which possibly cannot be accredited to either Gus or Cora. It was during the Prohibition period and Gus located a demijohn of spirits in his fence line. It was common practice for the moonshiner to place a cache, and then leave and give instructions as to by which post or brush the jug could be located. Gus quietly retired the spirits to the safety of his granary. There was no way then, even as of now, one could keep a secret from his protecting wife. Cora observed some prominent men searching the fence line. In her husband's best interest she smelled out the demijohn and delivered it to the search party. And to my knowledge, that was the only shady deal either one ever participated in, with each other or anyone else.

Times were changing as of then, the difference being the West still needed strong pioneers instead of retirees. They did not work by the dollar per hour. At Gus and Cora's home the chores of milking, feeding the stock, separating the milk and consequent feeding of the calves, and slopping the hogs was all done by 6:00 AM, when breakfast was served and you were ready for it. Cherrios and Corn Flakes were unheard of. It was hot biscuits, honey, and home cured pork after a bowl of mother's oats. The horses had been oated and you had them harnessed by 7:00 AM, ready to go to the fields. The coffee break came at 10:00 AM

with milk and buttermilk, donuts, or whatever. The
lunch break had not been heard of yet; it was dinner.
Ten minutes until 12:00 noon you could hear the big
Swede, "Unhook." The horses were unharnessed, kind
of like a "marathon change." You either washed in the
horse trough or a big double number three bathtub in
the back yard. There were towels and a big toothed
comb by the looking glass mirror. The "lunch break"
was dinner and then about an hour of rest and story
swappin', then back to work. Four o'clock PM brought
the milk, buttermilk, coffee, pie, doughnuts and a 15-
to 30- minute break. You were then prepared for the
next couple of hours. Ten minutes to 6:00 PM you
could hear the big Swede, "Unhook." The horses came
first and supper was really a banquet at 6:30 PM.
Then the milking, calf feeding, hog slopping, stock
feeding and the rest of the daylight hours were yours.
A big local siren would wail the 9:00 PM curfew.
Normally you were more than glad to oblige.

The pay at that time ranged from $0.50 to $2.00 per
day. When grain threshing came along later in the
summer the crew slept at the machine and breakfast
might start at 4:00 or 5:00 AM. These men were paid
by the bushel and could make as much as $3.00 to
$4.00 for a 14- hour day. There never was a dull
moment and work was the order of the day. We had
lots of hogs at the time and Sunday, the day of rest,
Gus would help me harness a pair of work colts to put
on the feed grinder to grind grain for the weeks to
come.

About the same time Anders Nelson, my grandfather,
came to the U.S. from Sweden, there were Nelsons,

Andersons, Johnsons and ever so many Swedes that
came to Grantsville, Utah. At the dinner and supper
tables there was always a story about a relative or
acquaintance and a peculiar incident. Big John
Anderson told about the first antelope he shot by
saying, "I missed dat dere son-of-a-gun wit da first
shot. Da second shot I hit him in da same place!" Big
John also told the story of selling one of his oxen
because Mrs. Anderson needed some flour and the
sack material to make bloomer pants. Big John told
Mrs. Anderson to hook him up with a bronco ox
because he could hold up one side of the yoke and
they would train the ox to work. The ox spooked and
ran off, dragging Big John. The critter finally tired
and stopped. Mrs. Anderson comes running up and
begins to unhook Big John, but he told her, "Unhook
dat blasted ox first," as he himself was perfectly
gentle. Some time later, Big John lost his wife to
some sort of illness. John was coming down the trail
kicking rocks, quite despondent. Gus met him and
there was an awkward silence before either could
think of anything to say. Gus broke the silence with,
"I heard you buried your wife." To which Big John
replied, "Yeah, had to Gus, dead you know."

The Family Cemetery

Its fences are broke, the crosses are too,
and the whitewash has faded with time;
The grass is o'er grown, the weeds have grown new,
the aesthetics sure ain't worth a dime.

But this is right where my heart wants to be,
when it's my time to make that last ride;
Don't take me to town, just set my soul free,
it is here that I wish to abide.

The patch on the hill is where my folks sleep,
their grandparents homesteaded this place;
Like pine trees and sage, their roots all run deep,
in this arid and wide open space.

They nursed this small spread, with hard work and toil,
and fashioned them a life of their own;
Their blood, sweat and tears are part of this soil,
this heritage goes clear to the bone.

So leave me right here, right here in this sod,
where my family tree makes its stand;
I wish to lay where, my ancestors trod,
on this hill overlooking their land.

No manicured lawn, nor graveyard in town,
for me when my life's journey is done;
Just bury me here, and lay my bones down,
and let me and this land become one.

25

Hair Cuts

Dad and my older sister and brother, Evelyn and
Pat, making ice cream

So he thought, instead of speaking,
for the first time in his life,
and then mumbled something softly under breath;
That was only heard by Stanley,
and his patient, loving wife,
and it almost got him quickly put to death.

A flat-topped crew-cut was the only way Dad wore his
hair for many years. I'm sure that style became habit
as Dad served on seaplane tenders in the South
Pacific during World War II and it just never changed
after he returned home and married my mother. I
remember sitting in the local barber shop waiting for
the barber to finish Dad's masterpiece; it was truly a
sight to behold. The buzzing with the clippers was
uneventful. Even the straight razor on the back of his
neck never really caused me much concern. But what
really grasped my attention was when the barber set
the manure-fork-looking apparatus on the top of
Dad's head in order to get the perfect flat top. It did.
It looked just like a miniature manure-fork with a
hairbrush handle. The tines were spaced evenly apart
and rested on his scalp so that Dad's hair would stick
up through it and the clippers would hack it off at the
appropriate level. It reminded me of a corn combine
running through a field of cornstalks at harvest time.
That manure fork was an absolute engineering
wonder. The barber shop in itself was this young boy's
nirvana, but I'll save you the grizzly details and just
touch lightly on the subject.

It was always a special day when big brother Jim and
I got to go to the barber shop. The whole place was
electric—literally—and was a sensational overload.
The red and white stripes trimmed in blue of the
rotating barber pole, like the mythological Sirens,
lured all who passed by to come in for a spell, even if
they didn't need a haircut. From the first step
through the open door on a summer day, the smell of
hair tonic and comb disinfectant smacked you right in
the proboscis. The unmistakable click and buzz of the

hair trimmers beckoned the next customer to take his righteous place on the throne of manhood as greatness was about to be thrust upon him. The enticing allure of shaving soap in a mug teased you until the day you could justify taking a razor-sharp straight edge to the peach fuzz on your face. The barber shop was a part of a boy's right of passage.

Big brother Jim and I at a tender age

One day, Mom sent big brother Jim and me with a handful of coins to the barbershop alone, armed with the specific instructions, "Just ask the barber for a regular haircut." Freedom! At long last, we were entrusted with the sacred obligation of going to the barbershop by ourselves. We were officially big boys. It was a sign decreed from on high that our

toddlership had come to an end; we were peeing with
the big dogs now. Big brother Jim took his turn in the
chair first, as it was customary in the tribal order of
cowboys for the eldest to peak the summit of
manliness first. I watched in awe-struck wonder as
the barber bestowed upon Jim the hair clippers of
righteousness and anointed his head with Brylcreem.
Then it was my turn. I took my place, the chair was
my throne, the ratchet-handle was my scepter, and
the barber was my servant. I was king for the
moment as I proclaimed my edict, "Give me a butch!"
Big brother Jim's eyes got big and he blurted out,
"Mom said a regular hair cut!" I didn't know what a
butch was and I didn't care. I wanted one. The barber
was all too eager to acquiesce to my request and
started in with the big shears. I was a bit put out
because the barber did not put Brylcreem on my hair,
but it wasn't until I got home and saw the look on
Mom's face that I realized I didn't have any hair left
to put the ointment on. It looked a lot like a five
o'clock shadow.

But even that trip to the barber shop cannot be
outweighed in significance by the time Dad took the
roaching shears to big brother Jim and me. Keep in
mind, the roaching shears were used for trimming
horses' manes; they were huge! I can remember
sitting on a homemade stool topped with an old horse-
drawn farm implement seat, on the large stone steps
in front of our tack shed, facing away from my
attacker. The chatter of the grandiose cutting teeth in
the Oster shears was unnerving at least and
petrifying at best. One didn't dare flinch for fear of
cleaving scalp from skull. Dad lubricated the teeth by

dipping them in an old Folgers can partially filled with diesel. Oh yeah, the combination of fuel and friction created a smell like none other and when he went to work on my hair, it smelled just like a spring branding. And hot... whew, when those cutting surfaces touched your bare neck it felt like the hot breath of the kiss of death. I don't remember what my hair looked like afterward, but I remember big brother Jim's... it kind of reminds me of what is left behind after a swather—minus a few sickle-bar sections—skims over a gopher patch on a third cutting of alfalfa.

Later on in years when my sisters were married and had children of their own, periodically they would leave the grandkids with the grandparents for a weekend. Upon departing though, the last bit of instruction they would leave with Mom was, "Don't let Dad cut their hair!"

Hormone Therapy

An argument with a woman
lit the fuse of Stanley's ire
at the yearly debutante and fine arts ball;
It didn't take him long to go
from the pan right to the fire,
and his poor embarrassed wife witnessed it all.

Now, Stan's domain consists of cows,
mainly Hereford/Angus cross,
and he's hitched to an educated lady;
As accusations hit the air,
it sure caught him at a loss,
when dressed down by Millicent Claire O'Grady.

Millicent is a buxom heir,
she's accustomed to the spoon,
puffed up like a cycling cow-elk in the fall;
The string ensemble was midway
through a verse of "Claire de lune";
when Millicent backed ol' Stan against the wall.

She blamed him for her portly shape,
and gave Stan the third degree,
about hormones used on calves to grow up strong,
She stood him up and dressed him down,
and said, "All us girls agree,
Eating hormone-laden beef made things go wrong."

"I used to model lingerie,"
she fluttered with some disdain,
as she grabbed another truffle from the tray;
The fact she knew the buffet line,
wasn't hard to ascertain,
and she swallowed several crab cakes straight away.

It was plain as day to Stanley,
what had caused her super-size,
And he was about to loose a brief vignette;
When his wife caught Stan's attention,
and shot daggers with her eyes,
that said you best shut your mouth lest you regret.

So he thought, instead of speaking,
for the first time in his life,
and then mumbled something softly under breath;
That was only heard by Stanley,
and his patient, loving wife,
and it almost got him quickly put to death.

He said Ral-Gro weren't the problem,
nor the hormones that she had,
what she needed was a stealthy matador;
Not to save her from a wild bull,
or a bovine that's gone mad,
but to keep her from the 'frigerator door.

26

Dakota Red

Dad on a young Dakota Red

*I hummed a cowboy melody,
a tune without frills or fuss;
And I wondered if years from now,
will they sing songs about us?*

Written by James F. Walker Nelson

In the 20s there was a film produced of *Smokey*.
Sound had not yet been added to the movies. I vividly
recall the words of Smokey flashing on the screen
after he had done away with the enemy: "Now get rid
of this saddle." After that film was was shown, every
kid in the valley renamed his horse "Smokey." The
"Smokey" horse of Will James kindles a spark in my
heart for the son of a thoroughbred registered as
"Handsome Red" back in the Dakotas and before the
advent of fancy horse trailers and trucks. A county
fair was in progress, an annual horse racing program
climaxing the event, with the final one-and-a-quarter
miler. Timing it just right, a light-weight young
cowboy who had been exercising the Handsome Red
stud galloped him in some eight miles just in time to
enter the one-and-a-quarter miler, which he won
easily. The warm-up proved to get the blood
circulating in the big horse and then a gallop, trot,
and walk back to the ranch to cool him off. The ranch
was in the cow business and never took to the racing
circuit as we know it today. The Handsome Red sired
some good hot-blooded/hot-headed horses. A local
livestock producer was on a cattle buying tour in the
Midwest the winter of 1948-9 (which many still
remember).

At the home of Handsome Red this gent bought some
steers and included a very good red sorrel two-year
old gelding in the pack. Four years later after
buffaloing riders, the cattleman approached me with
the fact he had a plumb good horse wasting away. He
would trade him to me, sell him, or pay me to ride

him, as I was horseback nine months out of the year,
with very little trucking or trailering on the job. After
getting acquainted with Dakota Red, we had many
enjoyable miles and he took to cow cutting like a duck
to water. Although I could not do a decent job with
the lariat, for I think a rope had hit his think-tank too
many times. I believe he had been head whipped.

Dakota Red was a good horse if used every day, or
used *good* every other day, or used *hard* every third
day, but could not stay inside his hide without use. I
loved that horse. The way it was as I remember, 'twas
the latter part of September. The Grouse and Etna
Creekers, the Gamble's UC, and Pop Elquist's CP all
gathered at the head of Bluff Creek along with the
Warburtons, Tanners, Kimbers, and all, for the
roundup every fall. Sea-grass ropes, manila, and sisal
a-twirl and swish; the noose was fatal. The big calves
were all neck roped and would slide to the branding
fire to be flanked and tied on all fours. No holding
corrals for miles to be found, the cattle were held up
by mounted cowboys in a big herd. The calves were all
marked and branded and returned to the bunch to
mother-up and nurse, and then we would usually
have lunch. With the cattle quiet and listless again,
beef selection, sorting and cutting began. Back on my
horse again, this is where Dakota Red stood out. He
knew what cow cutting was all about. Entering the
herd as quiet as a cat, he knew the critter I selected
and quick as a bat, he would have it in the beef hold
up from the herd. I think he actually held his breath
those few seconds and when the animal was safely
out, he would give a big sigh, then turn to the herd on
a thigh.

Mark Warburton, a tall, well-built man in his sixties, wore a pair of blacksmith-built spurs with the Crowfoot brand inlaid on the forged iron band. The piece of work had been done by a UC smithy at the Gamble Ranch. I admired them much that day and made the remark about them needing a big man to handle them. "Well sir," he says, "on this roundup I have seen a man big enough to handle them." On that remark he stepped off his mount, unbuckled them and handed them over to me and said, "See if they fit." Perfect, tailor made. *[Side note: One morning when I was in my late teens, Dad placed the Crowfoot spurs on my breakfast plate, signifying I had become a big enough man to handle them. That was a very memorable day for both of us. Andy]*

After getting too many school age children, we had to move to town and Dakota Red could not stand prosperity without miles of riding. He just had to go to the saddle horse sale and there were always eager bidders, for he was a handsome red sorrel horse. After this sale, he appeared at every sale for several years and at one time had to have swum the Snake River to get back home. Finally, the years caught up with him and last I knew he was faithfully, dutifully carrying a nice young lady.

I have had some very good horses, good horses, and mediocre, but never did I have a sorry horse. As of right today we have two with very good potential which probably will never be brought out. Trailers and arena professionalism now dominate the horse world.

Will They Write Songs about Us

A Charlie M. Russell sunset,
hung suspended in the sky;
As I watched my horses grazing,
with my cow dog standing by.

I hummed a cowboy melody,
a tune without frills or fuss;
And I wondered if years from now,
will they sing songs about us?

They wrote songs about the stampedes,
on Loving and Goodnight's trail;
And some ballads of banditos,
of outlaws escaped from jail.

But because we're not as famous,
it's enough to make you cuss,
I hope they will write poetry,
and sing some songs about us.

It's not right to seek for glory,
for the riches or for fame;
But I still can't help but to think,
we are special all the same.

Our lives aren't as exciting as,
McMurtry's Woodrow and Gus;
But it wouldn't be all that bad,
if they wrote songs about us.

I know, we don't chase the wild horse,
nor dance with Saint Elmo's fire;
We just dance with posthole diggers,
and chase after strands of wire.

These things aren't as romantic as
trailing longhorns through the dust;
So it don't seem very likely,
there will be songs about us.

The great cattle drives have vanished,
now we drive our stock in trucks;
We pass the rail yards for sale rings,
and dicker for a few bucks.

Nowadays we just do our jobs,
as modern cowboys, and thus;
As we shoe, we hay, and we ride,
will they write songs about us?

But then as I work with my pards,
and we swap stories and tales;
I see we're writing our own songs,
and our legacy prevails.

As we ride into the future,
living this life is a plus;
Seems there are some good cowboys left,
writing some songs about us.

27

Cruelty to Oxen

Dad at shoeing school, practicing on a bovine

Grandpa with his white legs and sandals with socks,
gives the mosquitoes something to chew;
See Junior with his dreadlock hair and Birkenstocks,
well... the animals are fun to watch too.

As you can tell from some of Dad's writings, he did
not subscribe to the modern-day trend of political
correctness and was not opposed to firing a shot
across the bow of anyone who questioned his thoughts
or motives. Dad was not know for his patience;
ignorance was not a valid excuse in his book. One of
his favorite targets at which he directed his
impatience was folks who accused farriers of being
inhumane to animals. Oh yes, they are among us.
Honestly, I can see where a person with no
information or education on the care of horses can
think shoeing is cruel. At first notice it can look
deceivingly barbaric. As I have explained to folks in
the past, all one needs to do is take off their shoes and
walk down the gravel road to appreciate what your
horse feels. But even that explanation doesn't
appease those looking for a special cause to champion.

For example: It was the summer of the big Idaho
Centennial celebration, there were parades, rodeos,
and demonstrations galore all over the Gem State.
One of the special activities was a commemorative ox
and wagon train traversing southern Idaho enroute to
the Wagon Days celebration in Sun Valley. It was
quite a spectacle as oxen and wagons took to the
paved highways; the dichotomy was amazing, with
convertibles and Conestogas passing each other on
the blacktop. The asphalt was hard and hot and
created a surface similar to a rough-grit belt sander
in a pastry oven and caused a real problem for the
tender-footed oxen. My guess is, the only person
around with any experience in shoeing oxen was Dad.
Therefore, he received a summons from some
distraught pioneer re-enactors. He met them with his

shoeing rig, his forge, and some ox shoes at a gravel
pit by the Perrine Bridge north of Twin Falls. A
shoeing table was not readily available and you just
don't walk up to an ox, throw his hoof between your
knees and start shoeing. So, Dad had some fellers
round up a few bales of straw to make a bed for the
oxen to lie in, then fashioned a Running W out of
cotton rope. One-at-a-time, he laid the beasts of
burden down and began to shoe. This was quite a
novelty in the rural southern Idaho area. Not many
people had seen shoes nailed on an ox, let alone knew
there was even a need to do so. Consequently, a good
sized crowd gathered to watch the show. Now, keep in
mind, the gravel pit was right next to a substantial
tourist attraction, the Perrine Bridge. Spanning the
Snake River Canyon, the bridge was a favorite of
motorists from near and far. Pretty soon cars with
license plates from all over the country were pulled
off the side of the road at the gravel pit. It looked a lot
like a convoy of Yellowstone Park vehicles, stopped by
the roadside to take a picture of a Yellowstone wolf
that is actually a coyote. *It happens, I have witnessed
it.* It was inevitable that eventually a member of the
SPCO (Society for the Prevention of Cruelty to Oxen)
would happen by and put a stop to this inhumane
treatment. It happened, yet their words fell on deaf
ears as the farrier crew paid no concern to their
concern and continued their work. So the do-gooders
enlisted the help of the local chapter of the Humane
Society, once again to no avail. The oxen were shod
and no longer tender-footed, the crowd dispersed and
instead of the farrier being cast into prison, tarred
and feathered, or scourged with a cat o' nine tails,
Dad was the guest of honor at a bar-b-que that

evening. In fact, because of his heroics, Dad was
asked to ride shotgun on the lead wagon through Sun
Valley as the wagon train's Grand Marshall.

I can't help but to think those were simpler days.

Thank You for Your Support

Written as a song by Andy Nelson & Kip Calahan

This is a song of ecological harmony,
one with a sympathetic overtone;
A song that revels in diversity,
we sing of symbiotic Yellowstone.

Everything coexists to the smallest fraction,
in Yellowstone Park, the circle of life has grown;
Even the paramedics thrive on the action,
so feel free to throw them a bone.

That's right, go ahead...

Feed the bears "Ding-Dongs," join the elk in sing-a-
    longs,
and ride all the buffalo in our resort;
Climb rocks from dusk 'til dawn, sunbathe with no
    clothes on,
the park medics thank you for your support.

Grandpa with his white legs and sandals with socks,
gives the mosquitoes something to chew;
See Junior with his dreadlock hair and Birkenstocks,
well... the animals are fun to watch too.

Trash collectors, tour guides, and the park rangers,
at times may get a little bored;
But the paramedics always welcome the dangers,
because somebody's bound to be gored.

It's fun for the whole family...

Test the waters for heat, give the badgers a doggie
      treat,
though your vacation may be cut short;
Run wild with the moose, sure... turn your little dog
      loose,
the park medics thank you for your support.

Yellowstone Park is the best place to hide,
from the cares and the worries of your life;
So just hop into your SUV and ride,
with your girlfriend or someone else's wife.

What better place to enjoy the view,
Than this land that progress forgot;
But for those who bring the rat-race with you,
It's best to just stay at home and rot!

So, enjoy your National Park...

Give the finger to the bikers, make fun of the hikers,
not everyone gets a police escort;
Drive your RV like NASCAR, drink like there's an
      open bar,
the park medics thank you for your support.

28

Friends and Associates

Dad, center, building a branding fire with fellow
ranch hands up Trapper Creek

Each visit we'd ride and revel,
we'd talk of memories and wrecks;
The time ol' Ben roped a pronghorn,
and nearly broke both of our necks.

Written by James F. Walker Nelson

Joe Carlson

The late 1950s saw this "Worshipful Master of Farriers" with quite a circuit and in demand from Layton, Utah to Boise, Idaho. I had done much work for Joe Carlson at his ranch in Albion and a friendship developed which we both enjoyed. Edith Carlson was a superb cook and if you put your feet under her table for a dinnertime lunch, one may just as well forget about bending over for two or three hours.

A building/housing boom was in progress. Money seemed to be the going style of life. I was called to come to the horse farm where the good all around Bar Bob horse was standing. I recruited the best horse holder I knew, Joe Carlson, and picked him up at 3:30 AM. We arrived at the new stables at 6:00 AM or so. A cool late May, very clean surroundings, a two-horse shoeing floor, a very cooperative trainer, and the lady there was obviously the Segunda. I want to give everyone his due, but Joe was one of the very few who knew horse talk. He could sweet talk a cranky horse into cooperation. The boss lady knew her horses and there was no way but hers. Her husband was off building another house and the trainer was new and eager to cooperate with us old hands. The trainer attempted to do the holding at the beginning with Joe handing tools. As the morning progressed I could feel we had to have other arrangements. I suggested to the boss lady if she would have the trainer keep Joe and me in horses it would help, and explaining as to how I had to maintain a clean working area, I put the scoop and broom in her hands. There was nice music coming from somewhere but no one ever had time to change the records except for during the coffee and lunch breaks. There was still lots of sun left the following day after trimming 40 plus and putting hot shoes on eight. One for the record book.

Glen Park

In 1960, plus or minus a year or two, Winslow Whiteley had some well bred two- and three-year-old colts, most by Red Dandy, a 1400 pound stud of the Willard Cranney Farms. The Shetland pony was popular at the time also and Winslow never did anything in a small way. These young horses needed some good attention and I was approached about gelding them. Also, they had been pastured on soft ground, which left their feet in horrible condition. The young studs had been corralled from time to time but never haltered. The old U.P. stockyard was the place, and then I had to recruit some help. Kelly Poulton and Ray Gee consented to back me up on the ground and Glen Park came with a big dark bay rope horse. The studs were corralled one morning early May, a cooler and nicer day could not have been ordered. Each stud was singled out to be headed down an alleyway for Glen to front-foot and deck. Kelly, Ray, and I would do the rest. Kelly knew exactly how to keep busting him 'til the air was all gone and Ray and I would wrap him up. Kelly and Ray would proceed with the nippers on the feet while I handled the knife and emasculators. We had other help from time to time but we four gelded and trimmed the feet on 29 head of big stud colts and about a dozen Shetlands. There was very little daylight left when the last one was turned loose, 40 plus. I have never heard of any gelding bee that can start to equal that day. I don't recall Glen spilling a loop unless it occurred on one of the ponies.

Bill Sullivan

Bill was a big Sullivan fellow with many a true story and one helluva way of telling them. I was getting the packstring in shape one early September at the Flying B Bennett ranch. Bill was manager along with his wife Marie. Warren Brewer and his missus were there temporarily. Warren's stories may have carried a little on the plus side but he had mushed dogs in Alaska, commercial fished, etcetera, and his politician father, owner/operator of a Stanley Basin Lodge, had half an ear gone from some kind of a dogfight. A big money-paying party unexpectedly contacted Sullivan about a hunt. Bill reached a former packing partner, Stan Tappan, inducing him to bring a packstring and give us a lift. He arrived on schedule but his string was in bad need of shoes and that put a double load on me, but I accepted it in stride. Those bare-footed mules needed no rasping, just a hot shoe to burn the high spots down. The dinner bell donged and I called back about having only one mule to go and I'd be there. Brewer takes the story back to Stanley and Ketchum, that ten minutes later I was washing up, which was true, but he did not know all I had to do was clinch the nails. The story preceded me and I was legendary at some of those pitstops. Sullivan and Tappan of course would verify his report.

Arch Marsing

I recall a certain day in late December; the hunting season was over on December 15th. A "good" fellow packer—heart bigger than a moose paunch—and I left the Flying B with thirteen head of horses, eleven

packed light to bring out for various owners, and six
or eight for the end of the road. It was a beautiful
morning at the lodge. Arch Marsing was my silent
partner. His bitch wolf dog had whelped two nights
before and he saved two of what he thought were the
best. He tucked them beneath his shirt, and letting
mama know where they were, we started up river to
an outfitter's camp at Meyers Cove.

Every two hours we would make a pit stop for the
stock and for the two-day-old pups to regain their
vitamins. I always carried a wool burlap bag over the
pommel of my saddle for sundry reasons. The
afternoon of that day saw a light rain which turned to
snow. We made it to Meyers Cove outfitter's camp in
good time but the mercury fell out the bottom of the
thermometer. We had a rib-steak dinner that night
with much yarning about the past season. The
following morning saw 10 degrees below zero and we
were packing up eleven horses. We had an 8,000 foot
summit to go over to a road, mail traveled, at the
division of Panther Creek and Morgan Creek where a
semi-truck would be awaiting us... you guessed it, no
truck. Lack of communication or leaving it up to
someone else was the causation of our predicament.
The road had been snowplowed out and we could hear
the water running under the ice, but had no way to
get our stock into it for a drink. We had tent, kitchen,
and all for us, but nothing for our stock. As the sun
was sinking I loaned my wool sack to "Whispering
Arch"; one pup had succumbed. The mother dog
nourished the other while Arch and I adjusted packs.
Setting up for the night was out of the question.
Originally, Arch was to go down Panther Creek and I

down Morgan Creek, but we decided it best to make a go for Challis and perhaps we'd meet our truck. What we did not know, the truck was in Salt Lake City loading fresh veggies for Shelby's grocery store. Fifty long miles later, non-stop, we pulled a pit stop at the Challis Ranger Station. The temperature was 20 degrees below zero. The remnant of the Forest Service personnel came out in full force to help us unpack, unsaddle, rub our horse's backs, feed and water them, and show us to a heated room. After about a 30 minute nap I was on the telephone and five hours later LaDell Handy was there with a good up-to-date pickup and trailer. He took Arch and his horses to Salmon City and then me to Oakley.

A Visit with an Old Friend

I could taste the antiseptic,
as I wandered throughout the halls;
Weaving through wheelchairs and walkers,
in search of a name on the walls.

Not the best place on earth to live,
But was now the humble abode;
Of the old U.C. ranch foreman,
the man with whom I worked and rode.

Ben was my teacher, my tutor,
and a real-life hero unsung;
The man who granted me the chance,
to work horseback when I was young.

Although forty years my elder,
he treated me like an old friend;
Taught me about life and horses,
and mentored me clear to the end.

They said, "He'll not recognize you,"
Alzheimer's had taken his mind;
The nemesis of golden years,
had rendered his memory blind.

When a cowboy outlives his job,
his horses get sold or just die;
Memories of the life he lived,
are all he has left to get by.

And when that is taken away,
he has few things left to live for;
I still wasn't sure what to say,
as I went to knock on his door.

I entered and hoped to see Ben,
just like he was back on the place;
Instead sat a shell of a man,
with an empty stare on his face.

"Howdy Ben, how are ya doin',"
I gently coaxed for a reply;
But he just stared out his window,
captive of a ceiling-tile sky.

I first talked of trivial things,
like weather, stock prices and tack;
He never even blinked until
I mentioned his quarter horse "Jack."

He turned his head my direction,
and his eyes began to glisten;
I talked more about the U C,
as he turned an ear to listen.

I recalled his days of ranching,
told stories he would remember;
Took him back to spring time brandings,
back to shipping in September.

I talked with Ben in weeks to come,
every chance I got away;

We'd talk of the meadowlark's song,
and the smell of freshly mown hay.

Of cattle milling at sundown,
and the waft of chuck wagon meals;
The taste of an old piggin' string,
or just how a good cow horse feels.

Each visit we'd ride and revel,
we'd talk of memories and wrecks;
The time ol' Ben roped a pronghorn,
and nearly broke both of our necks.

But, on my last visit I sensed,
we may not have another chance;
To ride the wide circle again,
or go to another barn dance.

So I began talking 'bout calves,
and starting colts in the round pen;
Then stopped gabbing for a moment,
moved over and sat down by Ben.

Well, he never did speak that day,
just listened, he smiled and then cried;
Grabbed my hand with a grateful clasp,
leaned back in his chair, and then died.

I often think about ol' Ben,
about how much he meant to me;
The life he lived as a cowboy,
and the day when he was set free.

29

The Taxonomy of Humans vs. Farriers

Taking a break with a rank one (left to right, Floyd
Judd, Uncle George Franks, and Dad)

About anyone can tack on a shoe,
but there's more to shoeing than that;
Like there is more to being a cowboy,
than owning a horse and a hat.

I've always thought it took a special kind of
personality to spend an extended amount of time
underneath a horse. I mean, what person in his right
mind would enjoy being doubled under an animal
that weighs at least five times what he does and
could, at will, have his way with you. But like night
calvers, port-a-potty cleaners, and the folks who
trick-test bulls, somebody has to do it. Luckily for
every horse created by God, he does not have to rely
on his owner to shoe him. If he did, there would be a
world-wide shortage of vet wrap, gauze, disinfectant,
and Quick Boots. Science has attempted to
categorize man and his ancestors, so we'll give it a
try with the mighty farrier. Grab your divining rods,
crystal balls, or the soothsayer tool of your choice, as
we explore the farrier and why he is, the way he is
by delving into the principal taxonomic categories of
the farrier versus the *average* human.

Human Kingdom: *Animalia,* distinguished between
animal, vegetable, and mineral.
Farrier Kingdom: *Ana-vege-min*, could not be
distinguished between animal, vegetable, or mineral.

Human Phylum: *Chordata* (Vertebrate), an animal
possessing a backbone.
Farrier Phylum: *Sore-data* (Barbiturate), an animal
possessing an arthritic backbone.

Human Class: *Mammalia* (Mammal), a warm-
blooded vertebrate animal that has hair or fur,
secretes milk and typically bears live young.
Farrier Class: *I'll-Mail-Ya* (the check), hot-blooded
vertebrates that have had much of their hair singed

off by the forge, drink milk, and look like they were never young.

Human Order: *Primates,* a mammal of an order including monkeys, apes and humans.
Farrier Order: *My-Mates,* monkeys, apes and humans kicked them out of their order.

Human Family: *Hominidae,* a member of a family of primates, which includes the great apes, humans and their fossil ancestors.
Farrier Family: *Done-In-a-Day,* a member of a family of steel benders which includes blacksmiths, farriers, and their fossilized joints.

Human Genus: *Homo,* meaning: Man.
Farrier Genus: *Slow-Mo,* referring to the manner in which most farriers move.

Human Species: *Homo Sapiens,* the species to which humans belong, Latin for, *Wise or Thinking Man.*
Species: *Slow-Mo Sufferins,* the species to which farriers belong, Latin for, *Everyone's horses have shoes on except mine.*

A little more on the subject...

Humans have a highly developed brain capable of abstract reasoning, language, and introspection. This, combined with an erect body carriage that frees their upper limbs for manipulating objects, has allowed humans to make greater use of tools than any other species of animal. Farriers on the other hand are best known for having a size forty shirt

accompanied with a size two hat. This, combined
with a bent over body carriage, puts them in a better
position to make greater use of the shoeing tools on
the equine species of animal.

Like most primates, <u>humans</u> are by nature social.
However, they are particularly adept at utilizing
systems of communication for self-expression and the
exchange of ideas. Unlike most primates, <u>farriers</u>
would just as soon water ski the Everglades donning
a ribeye thong than attend a social function, while
self expression and the exchange of ideas is usually
limited to, "should I use heal/toe, plates, or rims."

<u>Humans</u> create complex social structures composed
of co-operating and competing groups, ranging in
scale from nations to individual families, and social
interaction between humans has established a
variety of social norms, rituals, traditions, values,
laws, and ethics which form the basis of human
society. <u>Farriers</u> create complex accounting systems
composed of lost checks and un-mailed bills fostering
hurt feelings and borderline familial starvation
which form the basis of contention between them
and their wives.

<u>Humans</u> also have an appreciation for beauty and
aesthetics which, combined with the human's desire
for self-expression, has led to cultural innovations
such as art, literature and music. <u>Farriers,</u> too have
an appreciation for beauty and aesthetics, but
combined with the farrier's desire for self-
preservation, has led to occupational innovations
such as the hoof stand, the war bonnet, and Ace.

<u>Humans</u> are also noted for their desire to
understand and influence the world around them,

seeking to explain and manipulate natural phenomena through science, religion, philosophy and mythology. Farriers are also noted for their desire to tolerate or avoid the horse owners around them, seeking to either ignore or make fun of their idiosyncrasies through selective hearing, over-billing, temper-tantrums, and cowboy poetry.

This natural curiosity has led to the development of advanced tools and skills; humans are the only species to build fires, cook their food, clothe themselves, and use numerous other technologies. Though natural selection has come about through years of malpractice with advanced tools and skills, farriers are the only equine practitioners to set fire to their mustaches, cook mountain oysters on a shoeing forge, clothe the truth with fiction, and generally misuse other technologies.

Humans are led to the exploration of spiritual concepts such as the soul and deities. This leads to self-awareness, self-reflection, and the development of distinct personalities. Farriers rarely explore spiritual concepts; they know there is a God because there is the horse. This leads to self-abuse, bank account retardation, and the development of an unquenchable desire to own horses.

The Great Ones

The perfect farrier cannot be found,
but great ones are worth more than gold;
They are not judged by the outfits they wear,
or the pickups they drive, I'm told.

How one behaves before nailing the shoe,
often shows his level of skill;
And how he handles a nasty, rank horse,
measures a man's patience and will.

The difference is slight between great and good,
it's simply a matter of pride;
A seasoned farrier is proud of sweat,
perfection is burned on his hide.

They come all different shapes and sizes,
and from different walks of life;
But one thing that they all have in common,
is caution in using the knife.

There are shoers that still have flat bellies,
and can wear a big belt buckle;
Then there are the ones that wear suspenders,
and jiggle a bit when they chuckle.

They may be tall and straight or short and bent,
but the best ones don't show up late,
A level of trust comes through in his word,
and that's what makes the good ones great.

About anyone can tack on a shoe,
but there's more to shoeing than that;
Like there is more to being a cowboy,
than owning a horse and a hat.

He shows kindness, he has integrity,
and an honest love for the horse;
The great ones truly revel in their trade,
and the trade is their driving force.

The good shoers can always do better,
and fathers pass this to your sons:
The goal is to better care for the horse,
by learning from all the great ones.

30

Ol' Rap Scallion

Dad at the Flying B Lodge; the black bear on the
table is "Ol' Rap Scallion"

The shape of the moon is fading,
lunar light yields to the forces
of the omnipotent brush strokes of the sun;
I am summoned from my bedroll,
by the stirring of the horses,
and a new terrestrial day is begun.

Written By James F. Walker Nelson

If one were to sketch my short-but-quite-long life
line, it would have to be classed in these periods.

1. The Depression and Dust Bowl
2. The Era of the Great Bands
3. World War II (The Shooting War)
4. The beginning of the Water Well Development
   and the Pioneering of that Stage
5. Ranching in the Goose Creek Country
6. Horse Shoeing and Packing the Hunters and
   Fishermen in the Primitive Area

This all happened during Period 6., as a climax to
several years of playing cat-and-mouse with a bear,
the "rapscallion" in our camp, mainly the cook tent. It
appears to me as though the bear appreciates man
groceries, especially ham and eggs, bacon, wieners,
and most anything else. He has a keen taste for milk,
flour, and a complete disregard for utensils (these he
would scatter around the dirt floor just to hear them
rattle). So for several years this camp scoundrel had
been making a nuisance of himself. After years of
cleaning up after the bugger and losing untold
groceries—besides having to make unscheduled trips
back to the lodge for supplies, all by horse and mule—
it was my aim to put an end to the ruined bruin. After
watching Gentle Ben and Grizzly Adams on TV, it is
fairly difficult to make this a romance story for
followers of Smokey the Bear, but I grant you anyone
keeping camp and groceries and clean utensils for
hunters secure from this rapscallion was fighting a
losing battle. Something had to be done.

I arrived at this campsite with a group of hunters one early fall afternoon, only to find the cook tent a mess. A black tornado wearing a white bowtie had struck. Utensils were scattered, groceries a mess, and what had been Vienna sausages were crushed and the contents devoured. He may have entered by the door flap but he made his own back door. I'm only guessing this scene of the sequence that may have followed: A yard Raid fly-bomb can had been punctured by sizeable teeth and that may have had something to do with the tornadic tantrum which was very visible.

Four hunters who had accompanied me were on a limited time schedule, so I left them to unpack our string, telling them to do the best they could and I would see them sometime the next day.

I rode back to the lodge for another tent and more groceries, and also a bear trap. All other means of getting an obituary on him had failed. I had even slept out on the roof of our makeshift powder room with a flashlight taped to my rifle barrel in order to get a more strategic position, but he would not make a showing so long as anyone was in camp.

The Fish and Game along with the Forest Service had issued a proclamation prohibiting the taking of any bear within a quarter mile of any campsite or garbage dump, so I built the "Rap" a special pigpen a quarter mile and one step from the camp and baited his trap with fresh fish guts which I brought back just for him. It required a five-foot bar tied to the bottom of a tree to set the jaws of this trap. His pen was about six feet

by three feet by four feet high, with a big pine tree as
one end and a one foot log on the pen end for him to
step over into his trap to get the delicious guts, which
were placed at the base of the tree.

I have neglected to tell of his taking a bag of rolled
oats and some paper towels down by the creek about
100 yards from camp. He had to have carried the 100
pound sack in his arms and the towels in his mouth.

At the creek the oat bag was torn open and the towels deposited with big teeth marks in them. It appeared Ol' Rap wanted to wash up and dry before dining when he remembered he forgot to bring the cream and sugar for the cereal.

Now by this time the hunters were ready to depart with their game. The new cook tent had been put up and the camp restored. We loaded their game and gear and descended the seven mile trail to the lodge. There was another group of hunters waiting to take their place back up to the spike camp the following day. A change of pack stock and we were back fairly early the next afternoon. As we neared the camp, all hell broke loose. It took some plain and fancy riding to keep mount and pack-string under control. Ol' Rap had stepped in the trap and climbed the tree his chain had him anchored to. After some picture taking, I gentled ol' Ben with a 308 caliber. We were able to coax some of the pack stock into camp but there were others I could not get all the way in.

Needless to say, Ol' Rap's hide is nailed to the wall of the lodge.

Morning

My world is gently awakened
to the glow of a brand new day,
as the moonlight falls prisoner to the dawn;
Morning is quietly welcomed,
with the glint of a twilight ray,
and soon the shadows of sunrise will be gone.

The shape of the moon is fading,
lunar light yields to the forces
of the omnipotent brush strokes of the sun;
I am summoned from my bedroll
by the stirring of the horses,
and a new terrestrial day is begun.

But first I take some time alone,
while my senses are sharp and keen,
and I chance to imbibe in the newborn light;
The day is mine for a moment,
unmolested and quite pristine,
and my worries seem petty and somewhat slight.

Now I am primed to work my trade,
to the morning I say Amen,
and wait for dusk to reciprocate with dawn;
But like rain at the end of drought,
tomorrow's light will come again,
and the thought of a new morning spurs me on.

31

The Gag Reflex

Mom and Pat "helping" Dad feed

It had been a memorable day
for this local DVM;
With his one thousandth neutering
came the shame of all of them.

Why do you suppose God saw fit to install a hair-trigger gag reflex in some models of the human race? I'm not certain why but my mother Barbara was not one of those people.

My mother was amazing. She was by trade an emergency-room nurse and saw it all. Nothing could ruffle her feathers, nothing upset her stomach, and few things ever made her gag. She even witnessed a scene so gruesome that it would make the average man double over, wince in sympathetic pain, and dry heave like an empty windmill pipe. She worked the graveyard shift at a hospital twenty miles away, when one night an inebriated young cowboy, bent at the waist, shuffled into the emergency room and was greeted by Mom. Unable to make coherent conversation due to a mixture of whiskey and pain, the cowboy just moaned. The shift doctor was called to the not-so-private room with the bed-sheet partitions and a medical assessment was underway. It didn't take long to diagnose the problem. The patient history revealed that the young cowboy was to become a new father... again... and shortly after he was informed of this special announcement from his sweet bride, he decided to take matters in his own hands, *literally*. Not wanting any more children, he armed himself with a quart of liquid courage and an elasterator (elastic castrator)... yep, the mechanism that stretches out those extra-strong, little green cheerios (elastic castration rings) and allows the operator to place them over the maleness of a calf or lamb, thus cutting off circulation until the parts affected become necrotic and drop off. Even just telling this story still gives me a full-body shiver; the

poor feller must have had the Marquis de Sade
somewhere in his ancestry. He figured this would be a
good form of birth control but when even the
anesthesia of alcohol could no longer dull the pain, he
sought medical attention. The industrial-strength
rubber-band was removed, the patient sent along his
way with medications, and Mom didn't even flinch.
But after the young cowboy left, a good laugh was had
by all and she couldn't wait to get home and tell Dad
about the encounter with sadistic glee.

Dad, on the other hand, was one of those blessed with
a hair-trigger gag reflex, but only when encountering
a dirty diaper. He could pluck a cancer eye out of an
old cow, plunge his arm inside a gravid mare to help a
foal, or treat a bovine lump jaw, but he couldn't
change a diaper. He'd retch and heave at the mere
smell of soiled linen. This created a real problem
when Mom and Dad lived on the Wine Cup ranch up
Goose Creek, some forty miles on a less-than-
desirable dirt road from the nearest town. Mom had
to go to town for groceries and my oldest brother Pat,
still in diapers, was left behind with Dad. I get the
impression that Dad did not volunteer for the duty,
yet the mantle was placed upon him. Shortly after
Mom left, Pat soiled his knickers and Dad sprang into
action. He stripped the little boy of the fouled clothing
and proceeded with the Technicolor yawn. He
retched, he yacked, he chundered, and still could not
get the job done. So what did he do? Like any other
industrious man in crisis mode, he improvised. He sat
Pat on the pot... and there he stayed until Mom
returned from town. I have no earthy idea how long
that was, but the stories are told that when Mom

returned to the ranch and rescued Pat from the pot, he had quite a perma-ring around is his little tushy.

I, too, inherited a hair-trigger gag reflex and like my father; it involves mostly human bodily functions. I'm pretty good with animals. In fact, one summer while working for a vet, my strength was tested thoroughly. We were called out to a ranch to help the new owner with a mysterious outbreak of bovine abscesses that affected the whole herd, on the same side, in the same general area. Upon further investigation, we discovered the new owner to be not much of a cattleman. In the late spring of the year he decided to vaccinate his herd—*with what vaccine, we are still not sure*—but it was a nasty, rainy, muddy day. He ran the herd through the squeeze chute, and stabbed each cow in the ribs—*yep, the ribs*—with the vaccinating gun, pumping in who-knows-how-much of who-knows-what. Weeks down the road, each bovine grew a nice-sized abscess ranging in size from golf balls to basketballs. A couple of them were so big, we had a hard time getting them down the alley and into the squeeze chute. We then had to lance, drain, and flush the larger ones that oozed out gunk the color and consistency of banana cream pie. I held fast with not even a minor gag. With this being said, it is a wonder to me why I am a sympathetic puker. I am! All it takes is one small kid to purge and I'll go off like Ensenada, Mexico's famous blow hole, "La Bufadora." I recall once trying to clean up after my son Dylan who expelled his hotdog; my wife ended up kicking me out of the way as she had to clean up after both of us.

Chili-Dog Nightmare

Bob's conscience was a-gigging him,
like salt in an open sore;
His psyche was all but shattered,
couldn't take it anymore.

It had been a memorable day
for this local DVM;
With his one thousandth neutering
came the shame of all of them.

He slogged back to an empty house,
shrouded in a guilty fog;
Poured a tall glass of soda pop,
and made him a chili-dog.

As he polished off his supper,
devoid of hope and of joy;
Grabbed the remote and fell asleep,
in his favorite La-Z-Boy.

He wasn't long into slumber,
when ol' Bob began to dream;
He was sitting in a court room,
and a cat began to scream.

"That's the animal Your Honor,
my manhood fell to his knife."
Pointing a paw at Bob, he wept,
"I'd rather he took my life."

The room was filled with amputees,
equine, porcine, bovine too;

Dogs and cats all joined together,
to give "The Butcher" his due.

The recorder was a shepherd,
the bailiff was a tabby;
The attorneys were all jackals,
the crowd was getting crabby.

The judge was a Clydesdale gelding,
the wisest of all the breeds;
And there stood poor Bob in judgment,
for all his dastardly deeds.

He begged for mercy from the court,
but the jury had been mixed;
With some girlfriends of the plaintiff,
and others who had been fixed.

"Guilty" was the jury's verdict,
an eye for eye, the sentence;
"I'll never sin again," sobbed Bob,
"I cannot pay this penance."

Then Bob woke, and sang "Hosanna!,"
pledged, "My promise I will keep;
I'll never eat chili-dog,
before laying down to sleep!"

32

The Gentling of Critters

Dad with mare and foal, Gotch and Whiskers, up
Trapper Creek at a place they called Big Piney

I know how he felt, I've felt it myself,
while losing one close to my heart;
But how to explain the fact to a horse,
that death cannot keep us apart.

Written by James F. Walker Nelson

All the animal critters with whom I lived and shared
and extra baking powder biscuit may not have been
high school polished graduates, but they were gentle.
Prior to the first grade I learned that cows did not
paw calves out of the earth and rabbits may have
conceived in the cabbage patch.

We had a little part-Jersey heifer near to calving and
Dad said it would be a good idea to get her
accustomed to being milked by the time the calf
arrived. I would wash the bag with warm water and
one might say the little heifer was udderly delighted.
By the time the calf came the little cow had prenatal
education. We were still running both sheep and
cattle at this time and perhaps, as the saying goes,
living high on the hog.

I would make the final bed check of sheep with Dad
and the kerosene lantern. The lantern would cast
grotesque shadows particularly if there was snow. It
was something like walking in tall cotton. A severe
shock came when a ewe could not excrete her lamb.
Dad's hands were too big to help. He could tell it
needed turning around. With some soapy warm
water and my shirt off, he told me what to expect
and to attempt to turn it around in order for the
head to come first. With the good Lord willing plus a
bunch of exertion, we were the proud midwives of
twin lambs. The easy matter-of-fact way that Dad
gave instructions must be comparable to an airport
tower talking a plane in to land.

We had a nice yearling heifer which had been bucket raised and in the summertime we staked her out to graze the ditch lines. It didn't take long to decide to ride her to water instead of carrying water to her. I would ride the young work colts before they were big enough to put in work harnesses. All the critter animals were gentle by the time they were old enough to go to work.

We had some neighbors with a large herd of milk cows and an equally large family. We had gentled all their calves, ours, and everything we could corral. On the street ditch banks, five head of new ones showed up. They belonged to Tuff who lived at the head of Tough Lane, right at the beginning of tail-or-walk street. We would corral these calves and try to gentle them with our home-made riggings and spurs. 'Tis a good thing Hot Shots were not made then. At school Ernie Adams had a donkey that provided extra curricular activity and Dale Elison had an old switch-tail horse, which when flanked, could get some good gentling demonstration.

The common expression used for subduing a wild critter was to break it to ride, break it to work, or break it to milk. I, for one, deleted that expression from my vocabulary. I much prefer the words teach or train; please do not break anything. The gentling of the Calapucci horse Dad gave me all lay in the process of getting acquainted. Any animal critter cornered or scared will attempt to fight its way out. True enough there are outlaw horses but usually they have been made that way by some dumb man. When I started riding the Calapucci horse with a saddle, a normal cinch was too long so I substituted a work harness belly band in order to be able to cinch to the d-rings.

At any rate, Calapucci's name by now had been shortened to Cal and I was riding him all about the country and town. After a summer of feeding him sugar beets with greens, he would always come to greet me whenever I showed on the scene. When school started that fall I'd walk through the neighbor's field of sugar beets and pull two or three as not to disappoint the little horse. Then when he could see me coming he would lope out to meet me. Pretty soon I figured I would just ride him on in. So I cut me a rawhide thong from the hide I had been trying to cure (removing the hair by soaking in wood ashes and then in turn, soaking it in a juniper bark solution to give it color, texture, and to change the scent). I'd roll this up and carry it in my bib overall pocket so it would be handy to put around his neck and presto, my school bus horse was ready to give me a ride home. Dad remarked about the darn horse could tell time; he knew when four o'clock came every day.

The stock had to water from a trough at home and then go back to the lower field, which was left open. The field lacked a quarter of neighboring the school yard. One day Cal and the other stock were watering up when Dad saw him raise his head and prick up his ears and out he tore. Dad wondered what was going on so he watched the little calico pony go down the road and across the lower field over to the fence line as I was just crawling through. He ate his sugar beet bait and I put the rawhide thong around his neck and rode home in style, while the rest of the school kids had to walk and watch. This arrangement worked so well I'd keep him in at night and the next morning after a bait of oats, I'd ride him to school, take the rawhide off, pat him on the rump, and head him home.

A young relative bottle feeding an orphan fawn

Farewell for Now

Heaven knows why they were the best of friends,
they were different as earth and air;
Bruce was an eye catching Paint horse gelding,
and she was a Morgan cross mare.

He was my horse and she was my daughter's,
and they spent their days together;
A stranger horse pair, one never would see,
even if you lived forever.

One may not think that a horse can possess,
a way to feel anguish or pain;
But anguish was sure the day I found Bruce,
distraught, in a bitter cold rain.

He paced the fence line, visibly disturbed,
and nothing seemed to console him;
He whinnied and neighed, he shivered and shook,
emotion seemed to control him.

It didn't take long for me to discern,
what had my horse stirred up this way;
In the north pasture, lay the mare cold dead,
a lightning strike took her away.

I know how he felt, I've felt it myself,
while losing one close to my heart;
But how to explain the fact to a horse,
that death cannot keep us apart.

So I brought him in close, next to the barn,
where he was surrounded by friends;
Then buried the mare, on a sagebrush knoll,
not far from where Fayette creek bends.

If a person thinks a horse cannot feel
the heartache that comes with a death;
He's too far removed from the best horses,
to ever have lived and drawn breath.

Not too long after, the paint horse grew old,
now he's buried beside the mare.
I hope they have peace, wherever they are,
and a pasture they both can share.

I truly do hope, I'll see them again,
so I pray that God will allow;
For me to proclaim, to my friend the horse,
not goodbye, but farewell for now.

33

The Old Hide Ride

Taking a break on the Old Hide Ride with my
daughters Sadie (left) and Abby (right)

The night man calves the heifers,
and the poison kills the rats;
The only thing I've left to tend,
are those stupid, doggone cats!

Not too long ago, I was granted admission into the
deepest, darkest chasms of the female psyche. It was
a brief but terribly informative foray, as I was asked
to provide the entertainment on an all-ladies trail
ride. My quarterhorse gelding Blue and I were the
only males present on a particular afternoon ride and
I felt just as James Barton Adams described in his old
cowboy poem, *High Tone Dance*. I was a "burro in a
pretty flock of sheep."

The "Old Hide Ride" (their description, not mine), was
my opportunity to learn the "rules" that had eluded
me for over 20 years of marriage. I was about to be
enlightened and edified as we commenced our journey
into the Wind River mountain range. It was an eye-
opening experience as we rode single file through the
pine and quaking aspen trees. The conversation
rippled from the front of the line to the back of the
line like one of those steel-ball toys suspended with
fishing line that clack back and forth, back and forth.
I brought up the rear, but as soon as the conversation
reached me, it automatically reversed without
including me. This was not a problem as I was on a
fact-finding tour anyway and I witnessed this well-
oiled machine spring into action when the leaders
encountered our first obstacle. Across the trail lay
two, small dead quaking aspen trees and thus the
debate began, to cross or to go around. I knew I would
be receiving revelation shortly and I patiently
watched as this *machine* turned into more of a
committee, and the debate began. "I think my horse
will go over, how about yours?" The leader asked this
simple question and a flurry of responses wafted
through the air like down in a windstorm. "Well, I

compete in hunter-jumper competitions, no problem
here," said one rider, "I don't want to risk hurting my
horse," said another... "I think we should go around,"
"I think we should turn back," "Oh, put your big girl
panties on and jump over them," the various
responses volleyed like opposing teams over a
badminton net. The only constant in this discussion
was they were all in agreement I should not be asked
my opinion. Clearly I was an enemy spy and could not
be trusted. At last a decision was agreed upon... half
went over, half went around, the perfect solution. I
had the urge to rope one end of the trees and drag
them out of the way, but I was not privy to the
decision-making process.

Upon return to camp, a jovial mood filled the air,
mixed with feelings of accomplishment and self-
worth. Some made a beeline for the showers, others to
the make-shift chuck wagon bar, and yet a dozen or
so had not had enough riding for the day and were
probing each other for what to do next. Looking for a
little excitement to add to the day and bypassing the
filter between my brain and my mouth, I suggested a
horse race. I was not necessarily volunteering Blue
and myself for the race, but somehow it came across
as a challenge. I did not think through the
ramifications of being the only male in the race and
instantly three ladies accepted the challenge and it
was too late to back out. Deciding it would be prudent
not to race through the open meadow, for fear of
badger holes and hidden timber, the racers jockeyed
to a nearby team roping arena followed by a small
crowd of spectators. As we made our way into the
arena, an anonymous quote echoed through the

vacant canyons of my cerebrum, "The only
consistency in all of my failed endeavors is the fact
that I took part in all my failed endeavors." A sub-
committee then discussed the rules of the race to
make sure it would be fair for all and it was decided
that a sprint from one end to the other was the only
option. Hallelujah!... I was mounted on my team-
roping horse, who was accustomed to going from zero
to sixty from the roper's box to a steer; I may just
save face yet. Then came an intimidating tidbit of
information set adrift in my direction from one of the
lady racers. She was a jockey. I mean a real-life horse
racing fool. She was apologizing in advance because it
had been a few years since she had raced and her
current mount, a palomino paint, was a far cry from a
thoroughbred. Oh, the treachery, the deception, the
unmitigated gall! Oh ya, that's right... I was the one
who suggested a horse race... but nevertheless, I felt
betrayed.

Armed with the new information, it was not beneath
me at all to hedge the starting line as the racers were
lined up at the roper's box. Ol' Blue was cocked and
ready to pull the trigger. The signal was given, I gave
a deep, hardy "haaaaaaw" and Blue poured the onion
to it; we were in the lead in a flash. We were going so
fast I lost, in a cloud of dust, the hat I had pulled
down over my ears. We had them by a length. I was
feeling pretty righteous, but when we hit the midway
point I saw the palomino paint horse over my left
shoulder. Blue hit top speed about the point were we
usually head catch a steer, but that was all he had.
He's kind of like a bottle rocket: once lit he reaches
terminal velocity in a hurry but it doesn't take long

for him to burn out. The palomino paint caught up to us, then overtook us, and at the finish line had us by half a length. Blue and I came in second. To add insult to injury one of the horses behind us stepped right in the middle of my Atwood palm-leaf hat. That evening around the camp fire an awards ceremony was held and a plastic princess tiara with flashing jewels was placed on the hat of the winner... and on second thought, I'm grateful to have come in second place.

I had a lot of fun and learned many things that day, but I am ashamed to say, I still don't understand the "rules."

The Cat Wrangler

I wake up every morning,
and I go to start my day;
Run out to see the horses,
and fork them off some hay.

But my life of new contraptions
is enough to make you sob;
I've improved our place so much,
that I'm left without a job!

New tractors and new balers,
new feeders and the such;
Heated water tanks and hoses,
and a truck without a clutch.

Hired hands do all the working,
and it really makes me miffed;
That now I am dispensable,
if you somewhat catch my drift.

The night man calves the heifers,
and the poison kills the rats;
The only thing I've left to tend,
are those stupid, doggone cats!

I've become a "Cat Wrangler"
the worst thing you ever saw;
A fumbling feline caretaker
of fang and fur and claw!

The cats are my remuda,
I work them without force;
I herd them from afoot
and no longer need a horse.

I sew up tiny prolapses,
and help them birth and breed;
I took a special AI class,
a risky task indeed.

But I'm always extra careful,
to assure my health and strength;
I duct taped a welding glove
to the end of a stove pipe length.

I milk one to feed the orphans,
not the easiest of feats;
It takes twice as long to milk her,
cuz there's twice a many teats!

I worm and tag and vaccinate,
and write them in my book;
I brand and mark and castrate them,
save the oysters for the cook.

I've become the oddest catboy,
in these and distant lands;
But to change what I've turned in to,
...I'd have to fire several hands!

34

The Big Shooting War

Dad, second from the left, with fellow Navy men on
the shores of Mindoro, 1945

The way to pass this tradition,
and keep the values we hold true;
Is to teach our children the flag
is more than just red, white, and blue.

Preface

Dad was a veteran of World War II, or, as he referred to it, the Big Shooting War. The day after the bombing of Pearl Harbor, Monday morning, December 8, 1941, Dad was on the doorstep of the Navy recruiting office to enlist. He rarely spoke of his tour of duty in the South Pacific—and these are the only writings of his experiences—but he instilled in me and my siblings a sense of duty, honor, and patriotism. God bless the men and women of the armed forces... past, present and future.

Written by James F. Walker Nelson

Christmas Eve in the South Pacific, 1944; I was an electronic technician attached to a Seaplane Tender, mothering PBM (patrol bomber) planes. The mother hen Tender would anchor, if possible, in some sort of protected cove and the chicks would follow in and anchor, spaced irregularly about, for fueling and maintenance. The day before Christmas of '44, I was doing routine checks on radio and radar equipment. A motor whale boat would deliver the mechanics to make necessary minor repairs or adjustments and then gather them up later to return to quarters aboard ship.

When the Japanese made an air attack on the sitting ducks, their strikes always coincided with sundown and sunrise. They could approach at treetop level and have the sun to their backs. Radar detection at such levels was impossible and eye contact the same. It was not easy to get a ship underway and maneuvering to avoid torpedoes or the Kamikaze pilots. They did not disappoint us on Christmas Eve, but doubled or tripled their attack. I was witness to the attack from the wing of a seaplane and spent the night there. The Japanese were back at sunrise to continue their Christmas gifts.

The main difference between the Destroyer and the Tender was that our ship had a flat bottom to accommodate high octane gasoline for the seaplanes. Otherwise it had the same firepower, but not quite as much maneuverability. We did some convoy escort duty and shelling of beachheads for the landing ships carrying army troops. The most impressive was the beachhead invasion on Leyte of the Philippines. One cannot describe the fireworks day and night for eight consecutive days. Then we promptly did another convoy duty around the Philippine Islands and within sight of Borneo, to Mindoro, another main island near Manila. For about a month, one used his lifejacket for a bed on the steel deck. Very amusing entertainment would pop up at an instant's notice.

One day in 1945, Manila was liberated and I was on Northern Luzon aboard a Seaplane Tender in the Lingayen Gulf. We had pulled escort duty and contributed to the landing after the bombardment of Leyte. The convoy escorted 102 ships around Zamboanga to Mindoro. Countless airplanes were shot down, there were losses of ships, a-shelling and landing, beaching infantry, and come daylight there were only eight ships left in the Mindoro bay to provide provisions for the beached personnel. The next ten days saw continuous Japanese air attacks, (to this day I will not knowingly buy a Japanese product because I inspected a prison hold at Manila where U.S. servicemen had been incarcerated then incinerated). Back to Mindoro bay, ten days later only one of the eight ships was still afloat and on its own power, ours, the US San Pablo Seaplane Tender. That was due to the sleepless Captain Stevenson. We, the hands, napped on the steel deck at our battle stations. On one particular air attack I witnessed the bombing of our ammunition ship and the suicide bombing with a torpedo on its belly of an oil tanker. I felt the air blast from the ammunition ship's explosion on my legs and saw the smoke rise but never heard a thing above the constant fire of the 105 mm cannon. When the smoke cleared there was nothing but water where the ammo ship exploded, the oil tanker was burning, and a PT ship was grounded. This all took place in the matter of very few minutes. The helicopter was just then making its debut and surface rescue had to be done by motor whale boats. Many a trip I made with never a whale, but many spit-ups. One-spit up I'll never forget was a 16-year-old who was cook's apprentice on the PTB Tender. The Kamikaze pilot came sliding through the galley and the kid said he just had to kick his teeth in.

After the taking of Manila, Mindoro grew quiet, so our ship went to the northern island of Luzon, closer to Japan. The Japanese got their presents delivered the following August by Jim Doolittle and the B-29s that dropped the A-bomb nest eggs on Nagasaki and Hiroshima, which ended the shooting war. It was a great relief when the big "A" was dropped.

Betsy's Best Quilt

She's been around for many years,
this symbol of everything good;
She's recognized throughout the world,
yet is often misunderstood.

She is Betsy Ross's best quilt,
standing for pride and liberty;
She's held solid, faithful, and strong,
in surplus and in poverty.

She has witnessed countless battles,
triumphed where tyranny has trod;
Was there when a country was made,
and shows our allegiance to God.

She binds the thread of a nation,
an icon that never will fall,
She guides us indivisible,
liberty and justice for all.

She's been on every battlefield,
From Fort McHenry to Iraq;
She mournfully draped the caskets,
of brave souls who never came back.

Today freedom and tolerance,
together forever abide;
Where we go, our flag goes with us,
united, she stands by our side.

The way to pass this tradition,
and keep the values we hold true;
Is to teach our children the flag
is more than just red, white, and blue.

It's how we live and how we love,
it is in what we read and write;
It's how we work and how we play,
it's in the prayers we say at night.

The pride held in the USA,
by honor and respect was built;
We care for those around us and
we fly Betsy Ross's best quilt.

Shoeing Tool Definitions

Shoeing school at Cal-Poly, San Luis Obispo, 1957

No other melodic line can seize me,
or tug at my heart's very strings;
Like the sweet oration that resonates,
when my father's old anvil rings.

"Hand me the clinching block... no the block...
doggone it, not the clinchers, the block! Oh, I'll get it
myself." Being the young son of a farrier meant you
had the dubious distinction of being the tool-pusher,
the go-fer, and the fly-swatter all wrapped into one
job description. And if you were to execute your
duties in an efficient and timely manner, you had to
know the proper name (as well as nickname) of every
tool and in what order to hand them to the master.
Big brother Jim and I were Dad's tool-pushers, and
pretty darn good ones too, I might add. In spending
countless hours of boredom as an apprentice tool-
pusher, I had plenty of time to conceive and perfect a
shoeing tool dictionary for your edification. Pay
attention, I may need you to hand me the nippers.

Shoeing Tool Definitions

Hoof Pic: A small curved instrument used to clean between
the horse's sole and frog. So small in fact that it hides in the
bottom of the tool bucket until the farrier gives up looking
for it and uses his hoof knife.

Hoof Knife: A tool that is a close cousin to the carrot peeler. Oft times, it removes more skin than hoof.

ʊ

Nail Nippers: A multi-use tool not only used for nipping horseshoe nails, but most handy in the creation of blood blisters.

ʊ

Hoof Nippers: Often confused with the nail nippers when in a hurry, thus dulling the hoof nippers and creating an interesting flurry of adjectives.

Rasp: Used primarily for removing un-needed skin from your hands. Also used as a fly swatter on the horse's hind end, even if there are no flies present!

ʊ

Driving Hammer: A tool used in vain to hit horseshoe nails. This tool got me the nickname "Lightning," because I never strike twice in the same place.

ʊ

Shaping Hammer: Originally designed as an instrument to shape horseshoes, but has evolved into a type of divining rod that will locate the sorest finger holding the shoe.

ʊ

Clinchers: A tool used to push the cut off nails back out of the shoe, creating the need to hammer the nails back in. Repeat as necessary.

ʊ

Clinching Block: Used for the most part simply to irritate the horse by creating a vibratory tremor that can be measured at the nearest seismic station.

ʊ

Anvil: A tool used when the farrier needs a rest, all-the-while demonstrating to the customer that he is still working. (Strike the anvil with a 2:1 ratio, more as the situation dictates.) Also handy for shaping shoes.

Pritchel: A long metal instrument similar to a punch that is perfect for jamming in the nail hole of a shoe so tight that it has to be heated up in order to extract it.

Forge: Used almost entirely for igniting oil soaked rags in the back of your shoeing truck, as well as immediately trimming back facial hair (eyebrows included).

Shoeing Apron: Commonly mistaken as protection for the farrier, when in fact it is a public relations tool. It helps you explain to the horse owner that it is *your* blood on the apron, not their horse's.

The Dangit Tool: The closest tool available that you grab and throw across the yard as hard as you can while yelling "Dang it" at the top of your lungs! It is most often the tool you will need next.

Hoof Stand: A stand to rest the hoof on as you work. Intended to ease the farrier's burden but in reality the farrier ends up expending more energy just trying to keep the hoof in place.

The Horse: The abject object making all the above tools necessary.

My Father's Anvil Rings

No heavenly chorus or angel's song,
or pure notes that a songbird sings;
Can compare to the captivating sound,
like when my father's anvil rings.

No church bell on Sunday morn tolls sweeter,
such peace of mind the echo brings;
A sermon can't hold my attention like,
the way my father's anvil rings.

Beckoning to me like Homer's sirens,
the temptation frolics and swings;
The music lightens my burden of care,
each time my father's anvil rings.

No other melodic line can seize me,
or tug at my heart's very strings;
Like the sweet oration that resonates,
when my father's old anvil rings.

It rises above the turmoil of life,
as if lifted by angels' wings;
A harmonious tune wafts through the air,
as my father's old anvil rings.

The refrain cuts through the portals of time,
and softens regret's bitter stings;
No analgesic takes better effect,
than when my father's anvil rings.

As shoeing season again comes around,
a new hope eternally springs;
When the large hammer is taken in hand,
at last, my father's anvil rings.

I have no yearning for gold and silver,
precious gems to me are just things;
The rewards of a good life come my way,
each day my father's anvil rings.

Though my father lives no more upon earth,
he resides with the King of Kings;
Now I am the one that strikes it,
and how my father's anvil rings.

36

Some Gentle Man-Eating Stallions I Have Known

Dad on his way to confront Black Joe

Yet as the grass is cordoned off with fence,
I yield only to stay alive;
Because folks on the edge of common sense,
just do what they must to survive.

Written by James F. Walker Nelson

Cattle and horses have been my main interest for the
better part of my life. Being a professional farrier of
horses, plus some bulls, has put me in contact with
many ranchers and their livestock of all kinds. I was
passing the time of day with a fellow friend who had
farmed with and had been associated with livestock
in some manner all his life. The subject of horses
attacking man came up and he allowed there was no
such thing. I asked him if he had 30 minutes to spare.
We drove to Cranney Farms where at the time they
had something over 100 broodmares and nine
stallions in service. We are talking of a thoroughbred
racing farm. There were two studs one sure had to
watch and respect his distance. It so happened the
man-eater named Princely Host was out in a big
round corral for his exercise. When bringing this stud
from his stall it required two men with two chain-
shanked lead ropes in order to hold him off one
another and these were picked handlers. Well kind
sirs, he was cavorting in the corral making a
beautiful sight. I told my friend he was one to watch.
"Oh shucks, that horse won't hurt ya," said Floyd and
he started climbing the log fence. He did not more
than put his hand on the railing when about 1200
pounds of wild fury with his ears laid back, mouth
open and teeth bared, made for the man climbing the
fence. No attack dog ever looked as vicious. My friend
fell off backwards and was actually shaking when he
got up. The horse resumed his romping and when he
had his play out he could be led back to his stall for
feed and water. I was at the ranch one day when this
horse had rubbed his halter over one ear. It riled him

thoroughly. None of the handlers would get in the stall with him to attempt to straighten the halter right. Boss man Cranney came to the shoeing floor and asked would I come give him a hand. I was certainly not savoring the job but something had to be done. Armed with two hardwood clubs we entered the lion's den. Cranney was a strong and active man with a temper to match. The *Host* made a dive for him and was the immediate recipient of the hickory stick. Before the horse came to his senses, Cranney had him by an ear and I had the halter undone and back in place. Fast, short, and efficient we retreated from the den. I'm not sure how the *horse lovers* or *Humane Society* would have handled the situation.

Elquist, a neighboring rancher, owned a good irrigated farm north of Oakley and a lucrative livestock ranch in Nevada. He had an American Saddler stallion that anyone capable of holding a pair of reins could ride, but turn this stud horse out on the open range with a band of mares and you had something else. An elderly rancher from Grouse Creek was riding the range one day and unwittingly rode into this stud's territory. He was immediately contested and put to flight. The stallion pursued and poor Ernest Warburton had to abandon his mount and take refuge under a juniper tree.

When rounding up these horses it was essential for at least two men to go. As soon as the stud was roped, he was your kitten, then the other man could go for the mares. What most people can't visualize is what a fearsome sight these stud horses present when they come charging you, and they must terrorize your mount for he cannot outrun the demon. Odd it is to me that these gentle broke studs turn demonic, when I have never seen or heard of a truly wild mustang stallion turning on a rider.

The climaxing man-eater turned out to be a big black Percheron of about 1800 pounds, active as a cat and faster than greased lightning. Elquist needed some heavy horses for draft purposes on the remote cattle ranch. Mechanized vehicles were not yet very dependable, and Pop (Elquist) was not much of a motor mechanic. The big stud was broke to lead and was gentle to be around. Pop acquired him from the Gamble ranch, and still used the old UC iron which the horse carried. He was presumed to be from registered stock and he really showed excellent breeding. A band of mares of mixed breeding was put with him and turned out on the somewhat open range. The following year I was invited to bring my emasculators and help corral this bunch of horses for branding. As Pop and I approached the bunch the big black stud came out to greet us. He was not really hostile this time as he was probably just about four years old. We squalled at him and swung our ropes like we meant business and he turned around and proceeded to round up his harem. There was a wild-eyed mare kept threatening to break out but we had an eye on her. As we neared the corral she really made a break for getting away. I was quartering out to turn her back to the bunch when there was a black locomotive thundered past me. The 1800 pounds of Percheron outran me and grabbed the mare and sent her back to the bunch. Had I not witnessed the act I would not believe, and had Pop not been there I would dare not tell.

The following year Henry Callahan turned a mare in with the broodmare band. They were in a large pasture near the ranch house. In about thirty days Henry went up to bring her back home. He saddled up one of the ranch horses and went out to get her. He uncoiled his lariat preparing to rope the mare when here came the stud, and he had no intention of turning back. Henry was spurring his mount and over his shoulder was whipping the big black fury. The huge mouth was open and it looked as if Henry was going to lose his ass. The big jaws closed on the saddle blanket nearly pulling it from under the saddle when a piece ripped out and perhaps partially choked the old demon. Anyway he seemed satisfied and went back to the bunch of mares. Henry was still up in the front seat a-ridin' when he reached the ranch house.

Some of the barstool cowboys thought this amusing.
It is late springtime and this black locomotive is not
about to allow any, and I mean *any,* trespassing on
his domain. The bunch was allowed out in a larger
field. Pop was out riding fenceline checking cattle
and minding his own business and did not realize he
was in horse trespass territory when out of the
cedars comes big Black Joe. Fortunately the fence
was close by and Pop headed for it, bailed off and
rolled under the wire. It seemed as though mission
accomplished, big Black Joe returned to herding his
harem. The situation ceased being funny or amusing
to everyone but the town jokers and barstool
cowboys who would tell you what they would do.

At any rate, the situation had come to the point
where something had to be done. Elquist and
Callahan recruited me with my shotgun to either
corral or leave old Black Joe for the crow. We failed
to serve proper notice to *Wild Horse Annie* or the
Humaneless Society, or the *Sea of Animal Lovers.* I
loaded Ol' Betsy and we went out to accomplish
mission control. Let it be known these range-bred
saddle horses were not exactly TV stock. We did not
have to hunt long until we located our *quarry,* or
perhaps turn that around. Here comes old Black Joe
and he means business. Needless to add, I didn't
have to caution my pardners to stay out of my line of
fire. Our intention was not to maim the big horse but
to sting him to some kind of attention. When he was
within something like 50 yards I let him have a
charge. Well, all hell and damnation broke loose. Me
a-trying to ride my bronc and pump another
cartridge into Old Betsy; the son-of-a-gun was close

on my right hind quarter. I had to shoot that
shotgun as I would a pistol, but he was close enough
that time it gave him a-wanting a change of venue.
The locomotive came to a grinding halt, wheeled and
headed back to gather up the horse girls. I managed
to get whoa'd up, another cartridge pumped in,
which was no easy matter. We followed the big stud
and just as the engine was hitting a wash I gave him
a charge in the caboose. Harem, Sheik, and all we
headed for the corral. Let me state right here and
now when the gate was closed behind them we all
gave a big sigh of relief, especially me—no more
cartridges on Ol' Betsy. I had one in my hand and if
old Black Joe had made one more charge there is no
doubt in my mind it would have been one for the
crow. With a rope around his neck, he was just
another big gentle horse. We threw him and
fashioned a ring around his lower pastern to
interfere with his running, branded, castrated, kept
Henry's mare, and turned them to their home on the
range. Mission accomplished. Since it was so long
ago we should be free from prosecution today.

It would be unfair for me to leave you dangling in
mid-air, as to some of Black Joe's progeny. Some
were gentled, others never would accept
domestication and made quite a name for themselves
in the bucking horse world.

Do not misunderstand me when I ridicule the
Animal Lovers—I like them myself, I also like them
in their place—under your control.

Change

My office sits in the big wide open,
my job takes me there every day;
My duties of both ridin' and ropin',
are the only reasons I stay.

I work in the sagebrush and alkali,
from the comfort of my saddle;
Living the cowboy lifestyle and code I
care for my horses and cattle.

I try not to fight the prosperity,
take progress as it comes and goes;
Yet preserving lore for posterity,
I bend as the wind of change blows.

The challenge is to bend and not to break,
like pinion in weather's extremes;
I stand firm in this life of give and take,
holding fast to values and dreams.

Yet as the grass is cordoned off with fence,
I yield only to stay alive.
Because folks on the edge of common sense,
just do what they must to survive.

So I work this land like the men before,
that rode a free and open range;
While people around me tend to explore,
I cope in this vast world of change.

37

Things You Never Want to Hear Your Farrier Say

Horses awaiting their farriers at shoeing school, 1957

Then one day Knute struck it rich at the dump,
when a plum good boot caught his eye;
Perched perfectly atop a coleslaw hump,
just waiting for him to come by.

As a young man, I had an old farrier offer to shoe my horse for me, and he would cut me one heckuva deal. The deal was this, he would set one nail in the first shoe for a penny, after that the price would double for each additional nail. For example, the first nail would cost one cent, the second nail would cost two cents, the third nail would cost four cents... and so on. For the frugal investor, penny nails sound good. But let's do the math, 32 nails are used to put four shoes on the average horse. It starts out harmless with the first hoof costing you about $1.28, but your calculator will be smoking by the time the last nail is driven. After the farrier puts his tools away, you're in hock to the tune of 21.5 million dollars. Heckuva deal! That is one thing you never want to hear your farrier say... here are a few more.

Things You Never Want to Hear Your Farrier Say

- ☺ Ooops!
- ☺ How do you spell farrier?
- ☺ Fronts. Backs. They're all the same.
- ☺ What is the difference between a good shoeing job and a bad shoeing job? (About six weeks.)
- ☺ Now I remember why I quit chewing my finger nails.
- ☺ Experienced? You bet, I've been shoeing since Tuesday.
- ☺ What's your credit card limit?
- ☺ I took up shoeing because training was too hard.
- ☺ If the shoe doesn't stay on, it's your fault.
- ☺ I work until I have enough for entry fees.

- That blood is not mine.
- I graduated Magna Cum Laude from Guadalajara Shoeing and Taxidermy School.
- Dang, that nail never came out.
- If your horse hurts me, it's going to cost you.
- Try my easy payment plan, 100% down, zero payments, zero interest.
- What is your vet's phone number?
- The good news is, he has shoes on. The bad news is, I can't guarantee for how long.
- Wow, that hoof knife is sharp! Followed by: Holy cow, that's a lot of blood.
- I said a half keg of shoes, not a half keg of booze!
- I find it easier to just rasp off the excess hoof rather than shape the shoe.
- When I work I sweat, when I sweat I quit.
- I'm hoping to break my record and shoe your horse in under fourteen minutes.
- Too many hooves, not enough nails.
- Too many nails, not enough hoof.
- Would you sign this waiver please.
- Oh, I'm beat. You can finish this part yourself, it's easy.
- No, I'm not in a hurry. It's just that the warden said I had to be back before dark.
- I have the processing plant on speed dial.
- I find it saves a lot of time by using the belt sander and nail gun.
- If it don't hurt, you're not doing it right.
- Let's see, that'll be $75.00... Plus tax, handling, credit check, preparation, detailing, additional adjustments and options...

Knute's Boot

Knute's job was to drive to the ranch landfill,
in the boss's old garbage truck;
To dump the trash at the top of the hill,
and then return home before chuck.

But to Knute the dump was a shopping mall,
full of undiscovered treasures;
They were free for the taking, best of all,
fulfilling his guilty pleasures.

Then one day Knute struck it rich at the dump,
when a plum good boot caught his eye;
Perched perfectly atop a coleslaw hump,
just waiting for him to come by.

But after he searched and could find no mate,
he took the left boot to his bunk;
On subsequent visits he'd stay there late,
and hunt the right boot through the junk.

In the meantime the boot sat on a shelf,
in the bunkhouse above the fire;
For days and then months, it sat by itself,
like a lonely, leather church spire.

But Knute was convinced he'd find the other,
and kept searching trip after trip;
He'd dig and root, like a piglet's mother,
in refuse clean up to his hip.

When one day poor Knute was down sick in bed,
the cook did not know what to do;
Sent Ron to the dump, as he left he said,
"And take that dad-gum boot with you."

But Knute did not know his boot disappeared,
and on his next trip with the trash;
He found at long last the boot he revered,
underneath a soft pile of hash.

He hurried back home and into the house,
to find the other boot missing;
He chewed on the boys like a cheated spouse,
fussing and cussing and hissing.

He was stirred up by the dastardly deed,
and threw a fit to beat the band;
Then just stood there paying the cook no heed.
with one good *left* boot in his hand.

38

The Frozen Five

Dad (light hat), with family and friends on a
morning hunt

*The sun's hidden yet, my gloves are still wet
from yesterday's snow I didn't foresee;
I am miles from home and chilled to the bone,
and there is no place I would rather be.*

Written by James F. Walker Nelson

I am at a complete loss in wanting to be part of a
crowd. Our neighbor lady put it right when she
referred to me as being *anti-social.* One time after
herding sheep and goat hunters in the primitive
area, I went to a secluded waterfall campsite to
prepare for the regular season hunters. The job was
completed after two nights and a day, but I stayed
seven days more with just six mules, two saddle
horses and a dog and all the company Mother
Nature and Father in Heaven provided. Beautiful.
Back at the lodge I was given a reprimand, which I
deserved, but the private vacation was worth it.
'Twas still two days prior to general season which
involved baby-sitting hunters 'til the 15th of
December.

That particular year I got home the day before
Christmas and there was a big box awaiting me from
the Eddie Bauer company containing a down coat,
sleeping bag, and gloves from the Frozen Five. I
located these hunters who had failed to find camp at
1:00 AM on December 5th at 8,800 feet. We returned
to our prepared camp at 2:00 AM and you would
have had to have been there to appreciate their
gratitude for not being left 'til daylight some seven
or eight hours later. Never was a June bride given
more attention. They were convinced I was endowed
with some supernatural powers, them not being able
to find camp in the daylight, yet I was able to track
them in the night and bring them to a hot supper
and sleeping bags. One of their crew offered to help
me with the stock and the camp, which I graciously

accepted, so he stayed at camp keeping the big fire attended and the stew hot. After a fruitless day of looking for a saddle horse which had rolled off the trail, I had to take the inevitable task of taking a good, big gentle molly mule and tracking the rolled saddle horse to where he was wrapped around a pine tree. With the aid of the molly mule and an ax, I cut the fancy rigging of the Pro-Gambler from the horse, loaded it on the molly mule and proceeded back to camp. We had made much noise added with confusion so we elected to change camps. I drew them a map on how to hunt the next camp site, some 3,000 feet lower, in the next drainage. All but one took off on the fourth day out. I looked at my big, tall lantern-jawed helper who had stayed behind and asked, "Are you not going hunting?" To which he replied, "No, I am going with you!" After getting to know him better, he showed me his number 5 PRCA card. He was good help.

Doing Winter Work

It's windy and gray, a cold winter day,
out where the mountain pinion meet the sage;
The cows are callin', new snow has fallen,
my cowboy diary starts the next page.

The sun's hidden yet, my gloves are still wet
from yesterday's snow I didn't foresee;
I am miles from home and chilled to the bone,
and there is no place I would rather be.

I can see each breath, I'm froze half to death,
and my slicker crackles with each move made;
Equine hoofbeats sound, as steps hit the ground,
and we gather the cattle that have strayed.

The hoar frost is formed, as the air is warmed
all over my horse and some parts of me;
My back and head aches, my whole body shakes,
yet there is no place I would rather be.

The coffee is hot, and my bed is not,
at the home-place bunkhouse from whence I came;
But fence needs mending, and cows need tending,
and the horse I ride is turning up lame.

The work ain't fancy, can be quite chancy,
this winter cowboying on the UC;
I'll never have wealth, nor really good health,
but there is no place I would rather be.

The peaks are frosted, I feel exhausted
at the end of each day in the saddle;
Yet onward I go, through the wind and snow,
taking care of the horses and cattle.

The leafless trees sway, as I fork off hay,
and my Belgian team hits the double tree;
The tugs all keep time, they jingle and rhyme,
and there is no place I would rather be.

Then I ride some more, keep an eye out for
that gray wolf that has been hanging around.
I hear him at night, and just before light;
I've never heard a more bone-chilling sound.

Each work day is rough, sure is getting tough
to survive here in the land of the free;
Yet I always try, and barely squeak by,
'cause there is no place I would rather be.

I am most content, with the life I've spent,
entrusted with these cattle and horses;
I enjoy the work, and relish each perk,
and everything this lifestyle endorses.

As the flakes drift down, I don't go to town,
they really don't have a thing there for me;
To some it sounds odd, living here with God,
but there is no place I would rather be.